FOR THE LOVE O

MW01044510

"Michael Judd's *For the Love of PawPaws* packs between its covers everything you need to know to select, plant, grow, and appreciate this native, widely adapted American fruit. Be the first in your neighborhood to plant this tree that is both ornamental . . . and offers an exotic, tropically flavored fruit that's easy to grow. Read the book. Grow pawpaws."
—Lee Reich, PhD, farmdener (more than a gardener, less than a farmer), scientist, and author of *Uncommon Fruits for Every Garden*

"Get ready to learn, laugh, and get growing! Michael Judd's new book, *For the Love of PawPaws*, has it all: history, propagation, cultivation, harvesting, recipes, and even cocktails! Sit back and enjoy this wild romp through the sticky, aromatic, and delicious world of *Asimina triloba*, the PawPaw."
—Jill Cloutier, Sustainable World Radio

"Here in one slim volume is a compendium of information about pawpaw—the best I have seen. It collects the best info that is available online and offline, a huge help to pawpaw fanatics who are new to growing, collecting, and using the species."
—Neal Peterson

"*For the Love of PawPaws* is a welcome companion to the culture of growing, eating, and celebrating this uniquely American fruit. Michael Judd has captured the knowledge and joy of the pawpaw community."
—Andrew Moore, author of *Pawpaw: In Search of America's Forgotten Fruit*

FOR THE LOVE OF PAWPAWS

A Mini Manual for Growing and Caring for PawPaws - From Seed to Table

MICHAEL JUDD

The following fine folks contributed their amazing images:

David Eger, Earthy Delights: front cover top far left and middle images, the pawpaws in a bowl opposite title page, plus images on pages 100 and 112. **Jonathan Palmer, KYSU Land Grant Program:** front cover top right, the hanging pawpaw opposite the Table of Contents, Harry Momo's hand holding a pawpaw on page 30, and images on pages 10, 21, 84, 92, 93, 98, and 99, plus the split fruit on the back cover. **Lindsey Welsh:** the main front cover image of Michael and the family picture on page 9, photos on pages 150 and 153, as well as the right-hand image on page 151. **Kai Hagen:** captured our house image on page 8. **Elizabeth Somerville:** the cute baby picture of Avalee Flora on page 11. **Eric Baressi:** the popping pawpaw flower image on page 13 and the image of the baby pawpaws on page 76. **Neal Peterson:** donated the pawpaw fruit images on pages 13 and 88. **Todd Elliot:** the pawpaw bark weave on page 14. **Chris Patterson, Valley Road Orchard:** the whopping big pawpaw picture on page 36. **Aaron Elyk,** pawpaw aficionado: pages 86 and 104. **Alan Bergo, "The Forager Chef":** images of his great creations on pages 94, 107, 120, and 156. **Baker Creek Heirloom Seeds:** images on the front flap and page 96. **Leigh Scott,** whose food is as good as her photos: pages 101, 109, 117, and 118. **Ellen Zachos, "The Backyard Forager":** shared the image of her tasty crème **brûlée** on page 115. **Laura Davis:** the enticing pawpaw margarita shot on page 121. **Robert Bleifer:** the pawpaw fruit brandy on page 123. **Jane Deitrich, Bakers Brigade:** the tasty-looking pawpaw ice cream image on the back cover. **David Doyle:** the back cover shot of Wyatt Judd sticking his hands in the pawpaw pulp!

Unless otherwise noted, all watercolor illustrations © 2019 Nicole Luttrell.

Graphic illustrations © 2019 Tanner Csonka, except those replicated from © 2013 *Edible Landscaping with a Permaculture Twist*; the permaculture illustration on page 131, created by Karl Schmidt; the PawPaw Fest poster on page 154, created by Matthew VonHerbulis; and the "For the Love of PawPaws" art board on the last page of the book, created by Michael Fritz.

978-0-578-48874-5

Edited by Wendi Hoover.

Book design by Ponderosa Pine Design, Vicky Vaughn Shea.

Printed in the United States of America by Versa Press.

Disclaimer: Information in this book is based on hands-on experience. The author is not a trained professional in any health, environmental, or other field; he will not be responsible for the consequences of the application of any information or ideas presented herein.

This book is dedicated to Chris "Paw Paw" Judd
October 14, 1941 – February 5, 2015

Cheers, Dad!

Table of Contents

WELCOME FROM THE JUDD FAMILY OF LONG CREEK HOMESTEAD!

I have had the good fortune to live and grow fruit in many parts of the world, from the tropics to the temperate north, and I consider the North American pawpaw a favorite. Perhaps this is because the pawpaw fruit embodies the best of worlds with its tropical roots and northern hardiness.

Moving back home to the Appalachian foothill mountains of Maryland where pawpaws grow wildly and abundantly, I started planting select varieties of pawpaws. In five short years, big harvests were coming in and our 1st Annual Long Creek Homestead[1] PawPaw Festival was born. Quickly, we had over 500 people clamoring to try their first fruits. "Wow!!" The enthusiasm and excitement was palatable. I then realized we had a crossroads of culture and ecology just waiting to be explored.

Welcome to the pawpaw adventure!

Enjoy the colorful, diverse world of the pawpaw!

Michael Judd

July 2019

Long Creek Homestead

Wyatt, Ashley, and Michael Judd at Long Creek Homestead in Frederick, Maryland

---

1 On our homestead, we grow over 60 pawpaw trees, mixed in with black walnuts, American persimmons, and a whole host of uncommon, yet easy-to-grow, fruits.

INTRODUCTION

Would You Eat a Pawpaw?

The pawpaw is a cousin to the custard apple and cherimoya, the only member of the tropical sugar apple family living in the temperate north. Basically, the pawpaw is a tropical fruit tree that hitchhiked its way north as the continental glaciers receded at the end of the Ice Age. The pawpaw is now found growing indigenously, primarily throughout the eastern United States and very southeastern part of Ontario. This amazingly adaptive fruit tree has become so popular that it is being introduced into many other temperate regions of the globe.

The fruit of the pawpaw tree is intensely satisfying and nutritious. Indeed, it is challenging to eat more than one of these succulent—dare I say, heavenly—fruits at a time. The creamy, rich pulp has tropical flavors reminiscent of mango, pineapple, and banana that combine together to create a satisfying dessert. Pawpaws can grow wild and they can also be cultivated. The type of pawpaw you choose—wildly grown versus cultivated—will make a difference in how luscious and tasty a dessert will be.

Historically, most people have only experienced wild-growing pawpaw fruit, which can be a hit-or-miss game. That is quickly changing, as home and market growers explore the flavors of carefully selected and bred cultivars.[1]

This "How To Pawpaw" mini-manual focuses on growing, caring for, harvesting, and using pawpaws from seed to table. The accounts expressed are from my experience as a nurseryman, edible landscape designer, and permaculture orchardist, combined with extensive input from some of the greatest pawpaw growers and

---

1 Cultivars are seedlings that have been evaluated, tested, selected, and then named. They are propagated through grafting. For instructions regarding grafting, see Chapter 3: Growing Pawpaws from Seed and Grafting.

breeders—notably Jim Davis of Deep Run Pawpaw Orchard in Westminster, Maryland, and Neal Peterson of Peterson Pawpaws in Harpers Ferry, West Virginia.

Not a horticulturist or fruit grower? No worries. Foodies and chefs can glean information from chapters in this collection describing proper fruit harvesting, handling, and processing, as well as delicious and nutritious recipes that celebrate the pawpaw in its highest quality.

Getting to Know the Pawpaw Tree and its Fruit

The pawpaw tree has a unique, striking appearance with its large, lush, tropical-looking leaves and low-hanging fruit.

In full sun, a pawpaw tree takes on a beautiful 15-to-25-foot tall pyramidal shape, as shown on page 15—indeed, a spectacular landscape feature! It can also grow in the forest understory or forest edge; however, fruit production and form are best in full sun.

In the dense shade of the woodlands, pawpaws typically sucker to form in a patch. The height of the pawpaw in the forest varies depending on soil and light availability; in poor soils and low light, trees typically reach a maximum height of six- to eight-feet tall.

At the woods edge, with more light and richer soils, pawpaws can grow lanky: 15- to 30-feet tall with few low branches.

Wherever they are found, the huge, dark green leaves of the pawpaw tree are the give-away—at a foot long and half as wide, they are hard to mistake.

In springtime, with adequate sun, the trees blossom with nodding purplish-maroon flowers that are one or two inches across, before leaves emerge.

When sun and pollination align, pawpaw fruits develop. They hang singly or in clusters,

grow between two and eight inches long, and begin to ripen by early autumn. Trees with favorable genetics can produce fruits weighing over one pound, with sweet, aromatic, creamy-rich custard-like texture, filled with tropical flavors of mango and banana, with hints of other fruit flavors such as melon and pineapple. There's no guessing that this exquisite fruit is in the sugar apple family!

A Quick Backstory of the Pawpaw

The pawpaw has a rich and diverse history that spans more than 50 million years of evolution into current-day North America. Fortunately for me, this odyssey has been well documented in Andrew Moore's seminal work, *Pawpaw: In Search of America's Forgotten Fruit,* which delves deliciously and adventurously into the pawpaw's past. The following are just a few highlights.

Circa 40 million years ago the pawpaw tree began evolving from its tropical cousins and moved northward into current-day North America, slowly pulsing north on the tails of receding glaciers and in the guts of giant mastodons. The pawpaw has proven to be an amazingly adaptive species that has sheltered in woodlands and along waterways from the Deep South into our frigid northern climes, surviving extremely cold temps of -30°F.

Many Native American cultures, along with European and African newcomers, celebrated the tree and fruit, as is evidenced by city, town, and street names, as well as in archaeological records. Traditionally, the bark has been used as a durable fiber for weaving baskets and fishing nets, the leaves and twigs as medicine, and the fruit as a nutrient-dense food source.

Coming forward into early American culture, the pawpaw fruit is highlighted in the travels of Lewis and Clark, as a delight of Mark Twain, a favorite dish of George Washington, and a helpful food source for escaped slaves traveling north seeking freedom.

Today, the pawpaw is experiencing a cultural renaissance as we look back into history and the woods, as we begin to appreciate the slow and local food movements, and as we get to taste the benefits of select fruits from over a century of breeding.

WHAT'S IN A NAME?

The word "pawpaw" is synonymous for papaya in Australia and New Zealand, often resulting in confusion between these completely different fruits. Adding to the confusion: many dictionaries indicate an additional spelling of *papaw*, likely originating from the Spanish *papaya*. Seems a Spanish conquistador way back in the 1540s decided the pawpaw resembled a papaya—and it has stuck ever since! Further muddying the waters are the variable spellings: from *pawpaw* to *paw paw* and *paw-paw*. In an effort to pull it all together, there is a growing consensus amongst pawpaw aficionados to stick with *pawpaw* as the common spelling, and, ideally, "North American pawpaw," to further avoid confusion. As pawpaw great Neal Peterson points out: "If it were two words, then "paw" should be an adjective modifying a noun "paw," which makes no sense."

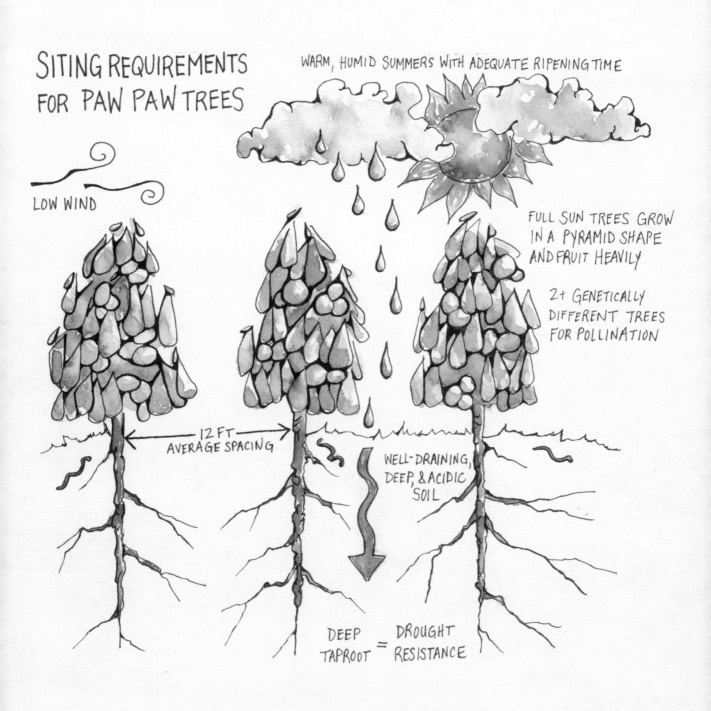

SITING REQUIREMENTS FOR PAW PAW TREES

WARM, HUMID SUMMERS WITH ADEQUATE RIPENING TIME

LOW WIND

FULL SUN TREES GROW IN A PYRAMID SHAPE AND FRUIT HEAVILY

2+ GENETICALLY DIFFERENT TREES FOR POLLINATION

12 FT AVERAGE SPACING

WELL-DRAINING, DEEP, & ACIDIC SOIL

DEEP TAPROOT = DROUGHT RESISTANCE

CHAPTER 1

WHERE CAN I GROW PAWPAWS?

There are four key elements for successfully growing productive pawpaws: (1) moisture; (2) fertile, well-drained soil; (3) warm and humid summers; and (4) cold winters that include some freezing temperatures.

The growing range of pawpaws is expanding every year as this versatile species takes root around the globe, from southern Louisiana to Europe to South Korea and Japan. In the United States, the pawpaw has naturalized over millenniums to a broad range that encompasses 26 states from Maryland in the east to Nebraska in the west, Michigan in the north down to Mississippi in the south. The boundaries of the pawpaw's range are being quickly expanded by intrepid growers into the Pacific Northwest regions of Northern California, Oregon, and Washington, and also the New England region, including Massachusetts and Vermont. Southeastern Canadian growers are also working with pawpaw varieties to fit their short summer season.

The pawpaw tree is an amazingly adaptive species that can push new limits. The fact that the pawpaw has traveled from the subtropics into freezing temperate zones shows how ready it is for exploring new terrain. However, despite its ancient tropical ancestry, it is thoroughly a temperate zone tree. It cannot be grown in the tropics or subtropics; cultivators have attempted to grow the tree, but have been unsuccessful.

When basic needs are met, pawpaw trees are one of the easiest and carefree fruit trees you can grow. Take the following information lightly and be ready to push the limits with where pawpaws can grow!

Even though mature pawpaw trees can tolerate temperatures as low as -30°F, they generally grow and fruit best in USDA plant hardiness zones[1] 5 through 9, fruiting where summers are long and warm enough to ripen the fruit. Fruiting in zone 4 is experimental, yet possible. This is discussed further in the "Temperatures" section below.

The original U.S. Forest Service range map of *Asimina triloba* was compiled from herbarium records throughout the U.S. Not all counties were recorded in herbaria. Although pawpaw appears to be missing from the Mississippi Delta down to New Orleans, in truth, pawpaws grew throughout that area. They now grow beyond the recorded native range.

---

1 See https://planthardiness.ars.usda.gov/PHZMWeb/

Siting Requirements for Pawpaw Trees

Full Shade to Full Sun

Pawpaws are commonly known as an understory plant found in the shade of larger trees of the forest. Despite that, shade is not necessary and, in fact, inhibits fruiting. In the heavy shade of the forest understory, pawpaws usually grow a lanky 6 to 30 feet, depending on soil, and often spread out to form patches arising from just one suckering mother plant. Understory trees produce very few fruit because of low light and the absence of another genetically different pawpaw with which to cross-pollinate. Pawpaw trees growing at the forest edge receive more light, reaching heights of about 15 to 30 feet and produce some, yet still limited, fruit. Pawpaws grown in full sun with adequate moisture, drainage, and protection from strong winds, grow into beautiful specimens with a pyramid shape up to 25-feet[2] tall and fruit heavily—with some cultivars bearing over 50 pounds of fruit per tree! See Chapter 5: Eco-logical Tree Care, for details.

Temperatures

Though established pawpaw trees can withstand temperatures as low as -30°F while dormant, they need warm to hot summers with at least 160 frost-free days to produce ripened fruit. In the United States, pawpaws grow in USDA zones 4 through 9, with most successful fruiting occurring between zones 5b through 9a[3]. In the colder reaches of zone 4, fruiting is currently experimental: the trees can grow well, but may not produce fruit. In mild winter areas with less than 400 chill hours, the trees also can grow well but may not fruit. And in the tropics, they cannot be grown at all.

Warmth is needed to ripen pawpaw fruit; there is no way around this reality. The tree will grow well beyond the climatic zones where it will successfully produce fruit, meaning you can have a lovely pawpaw tree in cooler climes, yet there will be no fruit to harvest. This plays out not only in extreme cold zones, but also in mild climates that do not have sufficient warmth to mature fruit, like merry ol' England and in regions with cool maritime summers.

WIND

Wind is not a friend to the pawpaw tree. Wind affects moisture, as strong winds will wick the moisture out of the pawpaw's large leaf surface, causing the leaves to shred. Strong winds can adversely affect pawpaw flower pollination. Very strong winds can cause extensive damage to the tree's branches. Exposed windy sites are not good for planting pawpaws.

---

2 Pawpaw trees growing in full sun can be easily managed at eight-feet high.

3 There are a handful of cultivars and regional seedlings that produce fruit earlier in the shorter and cooler summers. See Chapter 2: Choosing a Good Pawpaw Tree, for details.

Moisture

The big leaf of the pawpaw signals that it is adapted to humid environments; it needs a minimum of 32" annual rainfall or access to consistent moisture, such as a stream or irrigation. The pawpaw's deep tap root helps to maintain moisture needs once established in drier soils. Care and development of the pawpaw root is key in successfully establishing its drought resistance and productivity. Pawpaws can grow in upland areas and on slopes with good rainfall, wind protection, and mulching.

Drainage

Pawpaws need good drainage, as they do not fare well in water-logged soils. That said, pawpaws will grow in a heavy clay soil as long as it drains well. Pawpaw roots will easily begin to rot in persistently wet soils. These trees can grow along waterways where there is access to water, as long as there is good drainage; they often are seen on banks of streams and rivers, but not in waterlogged areas of a floodplain. The other extreme—sandy, dry soils—are not well-suited for pawpaws without supplemental irrigation and heavy mulching.

Soil

Soil should be neutral to slightly acidic, deep, draining, and, ideally, fertile. Pawpaws can tolerate a soil pH of 4.5 to 7.5, with a sweet spot between 6.0 and 6.5. Pawpaws have a deep tap root that likes a soil it can anchor into; for this reason, shallow, rocky soils are not ideal. They also like good drainage, so planting in boggy soils is not recommended.

Nonetheless, I have seen pawpaws grow in less than ideal soils and adapt to "rough" conditions. I have successfully grown pawpaws in infertile heavy clay on a slope, in flood plains that drain well, in up-slope forest openings, and in poor suburban and urban soils. Aside from soggy soil and dry windy sites, don't be surprised about the resiliency of these trees and where they can grow—remember, this is a highly adaptive species!

Ideally, a soil test should be completed prior to planting a pawpaw tree to check for pH range and any missing essential elements. See the Resources appendix for links to soil and leaf testing facilities. See Chapter 5: Eco-logical Tree Care, and Appendix I: Pawpaws and Permaculture, for my recommendations for creating the ideal planting environments for pawpaws.

Pollination

The pawpaw flower is considered "perfect,"[4] as it has both male and female parts. The flowers, typically, are self-infertile because the female pistils and the male stamens ripen at different times in the same

---

4 "Perfect" is a horticultural term for a type of flower.

flower. The stigmas (the female part of the pistil) mature first, then wither; after that, the anthers (the pollen-producing part of the stamens) shed their pollen. Thus, an individual flower is incapable of pollinating itself. Although the tree is capable of self-pollinating, this very rarely leads to fruit set. In practice, the safest bet is to have at least two genetically different trees in close proximity to each other because this is known to increase cross-pollination, and thus, fruit set.

Two different cultivars, any two seedlings, or a combo of a seedling and a cultivar, will cross-pollinate with one another. Cultivars are seedlings that have been evaluated, tested, selected, and then named. They are propagated through grafting. Seedlings are trees grown from seed and are not named cultivars. See Chapter 3: Growing Pawpaws from Seed and Grafting, for instructions regarding grafting.

Blooming takes place over a two- to three-week period, where each flower begins life in the female stage receptive to pollen; after a few days, the stigmas dry up and the flower morphs into the male stage, where the anthers release pollen—a truly bi-sexual species! The long bloom time allows

STINKY FLOWERS?

Contrary to popular myth, the flowers do not smell like carrion; rather, they have a very faint aroma akin to sourdough yeast. You really have to stick your nose into the flower to sense the odor.

for flowers to overlap, creating and receiving pollen. There seems to be no great variation in bloom timing among cultivars, so all should overlap in pollination for a week or more[5].

Pawpaw flowers are pollinated by ants, flies, beetles, fungus gnats, and humans. Humans have been very successful pollinators when conditions do not favor insect pollination. If pollinators are not active due to cold temperatures, windy sites, insecticide and fungicide use, or lack of ecological diversity when the flowers are open, then hand-pollinating with a paint brush can be easily and successfully achieved. Using a small, soft artist's paint brush, collect the male pollen grains, which appear as small, yellowish-colored particles on the anthers, and daub them on neighboring tree flowers with receptive female parts or stigmas. The stigmas appear as sticky, green and glossy tips of the pistils. Hand-pollinating typically has a very high success rate, so daub away!

If you have a wild stand of pawpaw trees that is receiving sun but not fruiting, then try planting another genetically different tree in close proximity to increase the likelihood of fruit set.[6] You could also graft onto an existing wild pawpaw tree to meet cross-pollination needs. For grafting guidelines, see Chapter 3: Growing Pawpaws from Seed and Grafting.

Do not use insecticides if you want healthy natural pollination to occur. Do put your compost pile in the vicinity of your trees, as it really can increase insect pollinator activity. See Chapter 5: Eco-logical Tree Care, and Appendix I Pawpaws and Permaculture for planting guilds that help with building pollinator diversity.

Spacing

In full sun, 8 to 10 feet is the average spacing for intimately pruned pawpaw trees; for unpruned trees, space 12 to 15 feet (with a maximum of 30 feet) apart to assure good cross-pollination. Tightly spacing pawpaws (as close as three feet apart) allows for them to be planted in limited areas where most fruit trees would be too big and spreading. In areas with high humidity and low air flow, give generous spacing to help prevent fungal issues on fruit.

Two pawpaw trees of the same age can be planted together side by side and will grow into what looks like one tree; this will allow for cross-pollination.

---

5 In Maryland, we have observed that late frosts can kill flowers, yet the trees can rebloom (albeit not as heavily) and set fruit.
6 Pawpaws grow well with black walnut trees!

Beautiful golden fall color of the pawpaw at Long Creek Homestead

CHAPTER 2

CHOOSING A GOOD PAWPAW TREE

While there are many well-known and noted pawpaw cultivars currently in the nursery trade, there are hundreds—if not thousands—more in the wild waiting to be discovered, and unknown possibilities in select seedlings.

Wild versus Cultivated Pawpaws

Pawpaws growing in the wild have a wide range of characteristics that run the gamut of fruit qualities—from small, seedy, and bitter to large, fleshy, and sweet. The difference can be akin to comparing wild crab apples to Golden Delicious apples—those experiences can be worlds apart. That said, many of the best pawpaw cultivars have come from exemplary wild pawpaw trees.

Unfortunately, many people only experience random wild pawpaw fruits and miss out on the pawpaw's full potential—a balance of aroma, texture, flavor, and sweetness. The good news is that there are a growing number of cultivars and select seedlings you can grow to guarantee top-notch fruits.

There are about 40 named cultivars circulating in the nursery trade. Mostly, these are selections of exceptional wild trees, along with a handful of bred cultivars. Choice wild selections and bred cultivars have superior traits that include large fruit size, balanced

Fruit from a cultivar (left) versus fruit from a wild tree (right)

flavors, firmer flesh, low seed-to-pulp ratio, consistent and productive fruit bearing, and ornamental value.

There are also "select seedling" pawpaws for sale in the nursery trade. These have been grown from seeds collected from cultivated pawpaw orchards that have no cross pollination with wild trees. Generally, select seedlings cost less and are a good deal for the home grower, as they come close to—or even exceed—the quality of their cultivated parents. Due to their genetic diversity, some select seedlings have more potential to adapt to regional conditions. Select seedlings are not grafted or given specific names.

For optimal fruit production, pawpaw trees sold without knowledge of the parents' genetics should not be purchased. If a nursery cannot specify which tree(s) the seeds came from, then it can be a crap shoot for the quality of fruit produced.[1]

Potted versus Bare Root

If you are buying pawpaw trees, you will come across two options: potted and bare root. Potted plants have been grown from seed in a pot, typically for one to four years. A bare-root plant has been grown in the ground, usually for one to three years, dug up while dormant, and typically sent through the mail to the grower. Bare-root plants are generally just that—bare naked, with little to no soil. For pawpaw trees, potted plants are the norm in the nursery industry, but a few well-known pawpaw growers offer only bare-root plants.

Potted Pawpaws

The ideal potted pawpaw tree is one to three years old and grown in a pot that is at least seven inches deep; a nine-inch deep pot (or more) is preferable. A deep pot allows for unhindered development of a long tap root, which reduces drought stress during establishment and will allow the natural growth of the tree. In short, don't be short with your pawpaw pots!

Most quality pawpaw growers and nurseries will have pawpaws grown in appropriately sized pots that are not more than three years old. To be sure, do inquire. I have ordered and received two- to three-year-old grafted pawpaw trees in just four-inch pots. Not good!

1-year-old seedling in a 12-inch-deep tree pot

---

1 Note that trees of unknown origin can be used as rootstock and grafted with superior selections. See Chapter 3: Growing Pawpaws from Seed and Grafting.

Bare Root

For nearly all fruit trees and bushes, I prefer bare-root planting, but not so for pawpaws. Bare root means that trees or shrubs are dug from the ground while dormant and replanted while still dormant. Typically, this happens in early spring and again in late autumn. Pawpaw trees can transplant well from bare-root digging, but it takes horticultural skill, quality plants, good timing, and special care must be given so the roots don't dry out. Pawpaws have a fleshy and brittle tap root that does not like to be messed with and often gets damaged when dug up for bare-root shipping.

Normally, bare-root trees are grown from seed in a garden or nursery bed and allowed to develop their natural tap and lateral root structures for one or two seasons before being dug up in the sweet spot of early spring for transplanting. If ordering bare-root pawpaw trees from a nursery, be sure to ask if they are

WHY PLANTING YOUNG AND SMALL IS IMPORTANT FOR FRUIT TREES AND BUSHES

When purchasing fruit trees and bushes, look for small and young, keeping root health in mind. For optimal plant health, roots should never be compromised by becoming root bound in pots or dug at a large size. Unfortunately, what is common to find in the nursery industry these days are large perennials grown in small pots with added fertilizer to compensate for restricted roots. Alternately, when large trees and bushes are dug and wrapped in burlap, their root mass is dramatically severed, compromising the long-term health of the plant—not good.

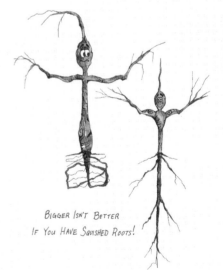

BIGGER ISN'T BETTER IF YOU HAVE SQUISHED ROOTS!

SO WHAT DO YOU LOOK FOR?

Young plants in adequate pots with loose and spread out roots will always have nutrients and moisture available. This is typically only possible with fruit trees and bushes one or two years old. Three years onward often brings root restriction and stress that will affect the long-term health of the plant, including its resistance to drought, disease, and insect imbalances. Seek small-diameter caliber on your single-trunk trees of a half-inch or less.

Having a healthy soil medium in the pot also helps enormously with good plant establishment. Most commercial potted plants are a sterile peat mix with slow-release fertilizer; those babies certainly are not reared for the conditions they are going to encounter in your landscape, as most fruit trees evolved from woodland systems need fungal-rich soil mediums and inoculants.

dug up upon ordering in order to assure the shortest period between transplantation. As a heads up, some nurseries will dig in autumn or early winter and store bare-root trees in coolers over winter and ship them in the spring. For many fruit trees, this method is fine; however, it is not recommended for pawpaws.

If you do go the bare-root route, be sure to add a mycorrhizal (fungal) inoculant to help assure good establishment and growth (see Chapter 4: Pawpaw Planting 101). See Resources appendix for recommended bare-root nurseries and mycorrhizal inoculants. See Chapter 3: Growing Pawpaws from Seed and Grafting for more details about pot sizing and styles.

What's a Cultivated Pawpaw? A Short Story

In the simplest terms, plant cultivation—or breeding—combines natural selection with artificial selection and cultivation. For example, if you lived a thousand years ago out in the Ohio River valleys where pawpaw groves naturally flourished, you would have taken note of those trees with big tasty fruit in abundance, and would not have chopped them down to harvest the fibrous inner bark to make footwear, baskets, etc. Rather, you would have cut down the trees with small, dinky, seedy fruits and fashioned some stylish pawpaw clogs, thus beginning the process of informal plant breeding.

Zoom forward approximately 900 years to the time of the early European settlers, and you'd find farmers who, while out hunting raccoons, discovered some impressive pawpaw fruits and saved the seeds and marked the productive trees. Back at the homestead, they might plant the seeds near the house or alongside the corn and tobacco fields. Over time, the best resulting trees—with good fruit and consistent yields—are kept and the inferior pawpaws are cut down. Among these selected prime producers, one tree really shined for strength of growth, balance of productivity, and fruit quality, so it gets named after a beloved aunt called "Matilda."

The reputation of Matilda starts getting around and by and by a fruit explorer, who we'll call Wyatt, comes to the homestead toward winter's end to see the famed tree. Impressed, Wyatt takes eight-inch cuttings of last year's growth from the branch ends (known as scion wood) that he carefully wraps in a moist cloth, and heads onward to the next rumored pawpaw tree of repute. In early May, Wyatt gets back to his property in Maryland where he has young pawpaw trees growing from local seed. He sets to grafting the collected branch ends of Matilda onto his local rootstock. Four years later, Wyatt is able to taste the first fruits of his labor. Although impressed, he waits and watches how the tree strengthens over another decade to be sure Matilda is stable in productivity, health, and fruit quality. Once Wyatt is sure he has a bona fide specimen, he writes about it in a horticultural journal and offers others to come to his homestead to collect scion to graft onto their pawpaw trees. And thus, a new cultivar is born.

It does not need to take a thousand years to breed a new cultivar. Neal Peterson, affectionately known as the *Mahatma Pawpaw*, has spent his life's work researching and creating some of the most consistently productive and tasty pawpaw cultivars available. Neal was able to breed seven outstanding cultivars in roughly 20 years, though, granted, he was using the genetics of his ancestors from which to launch his studies.

Breeders and Institutions

The interest in pawpaws has grown like a weed in the last 20 years. Hobbyist pawpaw growers, explorers, independent breeders, and universities are now developing new cultivars almost every year. Some are discoveries born from open pollination in home orchards; others are controlled cross-cultivations that are carefully monitored and hand-pollinated for clear parentage lines. The list of those involved in discovering and developing new cultivars is ever growing as pawpaw genetics offer much exciting and largely unexplored ground for adventurous fruit growers.

Cultivars

The genetics of different cultivars offer a wide range of variation, especially when it comes to fruit maturation and harvest. Some cultivars will ripen all their fruit at once within a few days, while others will spread out ripening fruit over a month's time. Some pawpaw cultivars will soften quickly

once harvested, while others will hold their firmness longer. There are cultivars that ripen earlier than others, which is an important trait for the pawpaw's cooler regions. Some cultivars have extra thin skin that bruises easily, while others tend toward splitting with heavy rains around harvest time. There are some cultivars that bear too much fruit, which affects long-term tree health.

Often pawpaw fruit size/weight is given in grams. To help simplify and save your brain from conversions, I will denote fruit size using ounces:

- Sixteen ounces is equal to one pound; this makes for a very large pawpaw, about the size of a large mango
- Eight ounces (half a pound) is considered to be a large size for cultivated pawpaws, about the size of a plump avocado

- Four to six ounces is considered to be medium-sized, about the size of a pear
- Pawpaw that are less than 4 ounces are categorized as small, about the size of a miniature banana

If exact information is available, the seed-to-pulp ratio is given as a percentage of seed by weight. Pawpaws that are plant patented are marked as such and can only be sold through licensed nurseries; all others can be openly traded and sold.

Note that flavor experiences are subjective, as even fruit from the same cultivar can vary in flavor depending on the region it is grown in and at what stage of ripeness it is consumed[2]. Fruit size is variable,

even on the same tree, and can be affected by site, climate, and soil conditions. It is wise to dig deeper past flavor profiles and into the consistencies of productivity, ripening period, seed-to-pulp ratio, and average fruit size.

Also note that ripening can vary depending on region, i.e. it is typical for the fruit of a given cultivar to ripen in Kentucky in early September and not until October in Michigan.

The following are well-known and noted cultivars most likely to be found in the nursery trade. There are dozens more with limited circulation, hundreds if not thousands more in the wild waiting to be discovered, and unknown possibilities in select seedlings. This is but a smattering of the pawpaw possibilities![3]

SEED-TO-PULP RATIO

Pawpaw fruits have multiple large lima bean-sized seeds about ¾-inch long by ½-inch wide. They are oblong, dark chestnut brown, and smooth. In a small pawpaw fruit, the seeds can hog up most of the space, leaving little room for the tasty pulp. A low seed-to-pulp ratio is a desirable characteristic in pawpaw selection and breeding. An ideal range is 4-8% seed per pulp ratio in a given cultivar. The image here has moderate to high seed-to-pulp ratio at approximately 20%.

2 See Chapter 6: The Art of Harvest: Fruit Handling and Processing for details on ripeness stages.
3 See Chapter 6: The Art of Harvest: Fruit Handling and Processing to learn more about how flavor profiles change throughout fruit maturation.

Discovered Pawpaws: Best of the Wild

These cultivars have been discovered in the wild and identified as outstanding specimens or choice selections from avid pawpaw growers.

Overleese

Selected from the yard of Mr. and Mrs. Overleese in Rushville, Indiana, by W.B. Ward in 1950, this cultivar of the pawpaw was selected as the winner of the "Best Fruit" category at the Ohio Pawpaw Festival 2011. The Overleese is the "mother" of many excellent offspring, including the famed "Shenandoah," (see more on the Shenandoah later in this chapter). The large-sized fruit is a long-proven favorite for steady productivity, has a low seed-to-pulp ratio, and offers a moderate holding quality. The Overleese is an early- to mid-season producer of large fruits with medium productivity. Its fruit is oval or round in shape, and produces a mild-flavored, creamy yellow-orange pulp. The lighter flavor is appreciated by those not wanting the richer notes produced by some of the other cultivars.

A basket full of select pawpaw cultivars from the Long Creek Homestead food forest

Davis

Discovered in the Michigan woods by Corwin Davis in 1959, this moderate bearer is an attractive tree. In fact, the Davis cultivar is one of the most attractive pawpaw trees in my own personal collection, with a full, handsome growth and deep green leaves. Davis makes for a good edible landscape—an all-star among pawpaws!

Some of the excellent traits of the Davis include: the medium-sized fruits yield a light-yellow flesh that gives way to an attractive green fruit when ripened; it keeps well in cold storage; and the pleasant flavor is sweet and mild.

NC-1

NC-1 is a hybrid seedling of Overleese and Davis—also known as "Campbell's #1"—and was selected in Ontario, Canada, in 1976 by R. Douglas Campbell. This is one of the best cultivars for northern regions or regions with cooler summers, as it is an early bearer; it also grows well throughout the southern range.[4] NC-1 is one of the most ornamental of the pawpaw trees. Its attractive, dark green foliage gives way to round or oval fruit resembling the Overleese, with a low seed-to-pulp ratio and good holding quality. NC-1 produces large-sized fruit in low to moderate quantities. It has a firm fruit texture with excellent flavor and buttery yellow pulp.

Mango[5]

A strong-growing and productive cultivar prized for its light and sweet flavored pulp the Mango pawpaw was discovered from the wild in Georgia by Major C. Collins, circa 1970. The Mango pawpaw fruits are large and round, resembling mangoes, with a soft and creamy texture. The fruits do not store as well as most other named cultivars, quickly turning mushy upon harvest; for this reason, the Mango is a cultivar best suited to fresh eating or immediate pulping. This tree produces large-sized fruits and is preferred by those not into the rich and complex flavors of some pawpaw cultivars.

Sunflower

One of the most popular and recommended cultivars, the Sunflower cultivar is a staple in any collection. This strong-grower was discovered in the Kansas wild by Milo Gibson, circa 1970. Sweet and rich with a golden-yellow pulp and firm texture with few, yet large, seeds, this pawpaw ripens mid- to late-season, so it may not be best suited for extreme northern growers. This amazing cultivar produces large-sized fruit

---

4 There are certain varieties and select seedlings that will ripen earlier in northern ranges where the growing season is shorter, and in regions with cool summers that need more heat to ripen the fruit.

5 Mango has proven to be a strong grower in our food forests, with steady fruit set and productivity even at an early age. It will grow large if not pruned.

and is self-fertile; given this, it is always best to plant more than one cultivar or seedling to improve fruit set. The Sunflower tested high in the Cornell University trials[6] and won best fruit at the Ohio Pawpaw Festival both in 2006 and 2010.

Pennsylvania Golden

Often abbreviated as "PA Golden," this cultivar is famed for its early and heavy production. It is a top-choice cultivar for the northern reaches, plus regions with shorter growing seasons and cooler summers, yet it grows well in warm areas, too. The seeds were elected by John Gordon of New York from trees that trace back to George A. Zimmerman, a famed pawpaw culturist in the 1920s and 1930s. There are four PA Goldens, known as the "PA Series." The series is identified as PA Golden #1, #2, #3, and #4, with #1 and #4 being the most common in the nursery industry. They are all early ripening and a must-have for any collection living in a climate with a short growing season.

The PA Golden has deep golden pulp with a creamy, somewhat watery, texture and rich flavor. Many consumers prefer this richness, while others find it to be too strong. The softer texture means the fruit does not store well and is best eaten fresh or pulped quickly.

I find the PA Goldens to resemble wild pawpaws in many ways: smaller, seedy, and sometimes with slight bitter undertones. That said, it is a great growing, very hardy, and productive tree whose small-to-medium sized fruit turn yellow when ripe, making harvest time obvious.

MORE, MORE, MORE!

There are many more wild and selected cultivars than this list of my personal favorites. I encourage you to check with the nurseries listed in the Resources section to see what is available in the trade and engage with the extensive online pawpaw community to get firsthand accounts of cultivar qualities and performance.

Over the years, many pawpaw varieties have been named and released by amateur explorers or growers that do not compare well with the better modern cultivars. This happens through a lack of adequate testing and evaluation. There are a few selected cultivars that I would not include in a limited collection, namely Wells, Prolific, Wilson, Middletown, and Mitchell.

If you live in the pawpaw's extended growing range, you are best off checking with regional nurseries to find out what is growing best in your set of conditions. Don't be surprised if they recommend an unnamed selection that has proven itself in their trials—ultimately it's not all about the cultivars!

---

6 Starting in 1999 Cornell University, located in Ithaca, New York, participated in a regional varietal trial consisting of 28 commercially available pawpaw varieties to evaluate adaptability for cool, humid fruit-growing regions.

Sue

Discovered by Don Munich in southern Indiana. The Sue cultivar is known for its sweetness. Jim Davis, owner and operator of Deep Run Pawpaw Orchard in Westminster, Maryland, agrees, as the Sue is sweet and simple, ideal for those who don't go for the stronger pawpaw flavors. The small- to medium-sized fruit produces a soft, yellow pulp that makes for a sweet creamy dessert. Sue's thin skin turns yellow when ripe and is a good producer. Multiple records indicate the Sue to be resistant to *Phyllosticta asminae*[7], a fungus that often discolors the skin of pawpaw fruit with black spots and blotches.

Ford Amend

The Ford Amend merits mention as a pawpaw selected in the Northwest region of the United States where summers are not extremely hot. Grown successfully since the 1950s and still being sold in the nursery trade, this version yields small- to medium-sized fruit offering a flavorful orange pulp. It matures in late September in Oregon and neighboring states.

Summer's Delight and Halvin's Sidewinder

These two cultivars are newer releases with promises to explore.

Bred Cultivars

The following are the results of meticulous research, thorough and careful genetic cataloging, and extensive trials.

PETERSON PAWPAWS

Neal Peterson is the breeder of seven cultivars, collectively known as "Petersons Pawpaws." They are named after U.S. rivers with Native American names. The short story[8] is that Neal tracked down the historic pawpaw collections from a century ago when pawpaws were revered and celebrated. Roughly 1,500 seedlings grew out of this collection, which Neal evaluated over a 20-year period. He selected the very best, finally narrowing it down to just seven outstanding cultivars: Shenandoah, Allegheny, Susquehanna, Potomac, Rappahannock, Wabash, and Tallahatchie. Detail on each cultivar follows.

Neal's dedicated work has created cultivars with desirable characteristics in flavor, texture, size, seed-to-pulp ratio, and productivity. When you grow a Peterson Pawpaw, you know what to look forward to. Neal is currently working on spreading his cultivars around the world.

---

7 See Chapter 5: Eco-logical Tree Care for information regarding *Phyllosticta asminae.*
8 Neal's pawpaw story and life's work is worth exploring in more detail. I recommend reading Andrew Moore's book, *Pawpaw: In Search of America's Forgotten Fruit,* to learn more about Neal and other pawpaw greats. Neal's website is a fabulous resource for everything pawpaw: www.petersonpawpaws.com.

Shenandoah

The "Queen" of Peterson's Pawpaws, the Shenandoah has a long list of fine attributes. It is a very steady producer of large fruits with few seeds and a spaced-out ripening period that can stretch over a month's time in mid-season. Shenandoah often bears a single fruit rather than a cluster, which makes picking fruit much easier and reduces potential fungal build-up that can occur between clustered fruits, which have a fragrant, sweet flavor, a custardy texture, and a smooth aftertaste. Shenandoah is a good first pawpaw fruit to try, as it is on the light, sweet side of the pawpaw-flavor spectrum. It is a long-proven producer at Jim Davis's Deep Run Pawpaw Orchard. (6% seed by weight)

Allegheny

The Allegheny is a personal favorite of mine for its strong growth, abundant fruiting, and balanced flavors. Neal almost did not release this one due to its smaller fruit size and higher seed-to-fruit ratio; however, he relented to popular pressure, thank heavens! The Allegheny produces fruits that have a medium-smooth texture with yellow pulp that is sweet and rich, providing a hint of citrus. This is a very precocious and productive cultivar that needs to be well-managed; the fruit should be thinned out as it has a tendency to overbear, which on any fruit tree can lead to overall decline in tree vigor and fruit quality. The tree is a mid-season producer of medium-sized fruit that grows in clusters—two or three per bunch with a limited number of clusters per branch. Thirty-five pounds per tree (for any pawpaw) is a good goal in order to keep tree health in balance. The Allegheny is another steady producer in Jim Davis's Deep Run Pawpaw Orchard. (8% seed by weight)

Susquehanna

This cultivar is Neal's personal favorite. This is a beautiful, large, plump fruit with rich yellow to orange flesh that is very sweet with rich, complex flavor notes and a firm buttery melting texture resembling Hass avocado. The Susquehanna produces consistently big fruit, often over a pound, with very few seeds. It ripens later in the season, developing a relatively thick skin that improves storage and the ability for shipping. The Susquehanna has excellent, healthy-looking foliage, so mark this one down as another Edible Landscape All-star! (3% seed by weight)

Potomac

The biggest fruit of Neal's releases, the Potomac's fruit provides lots of pulp with few seeds. Harvesting fruit this big is exciting; however, the down side is that these plump fruits can split if grown in areas high in *Phyllosticta asminae* or with heavy rains around harvest. This mid-to-late season producer offers a sweet and rich flavor with a medium-yellow pulp and firm texture. The Potomac tree has a strong apical dominance, meaning it tends to grow more upright rather than spreading. Jim Davis has long been a fan

A 2.2 pound Peterson Pawpaw harvested by Chris Patterson of Valley Road Orchard in Lancaster Pennsylvania

of Neal Peterson's Potomac cultivar, harvesting fruits as large as 2.1 pounds at his Deep Run Pawpaw Orchard! (4% seed by weight)

Rappahannock

Distinctive among pawpaw trees for its horizontally held leaves and symmetrical shape—a nice feature for pawpaw fruit picking—the Rappanhannock cultivar offers growers an early season harvest! The skin will turn a yellowish-green color when ripe. This small- to medium-sized fruit is of good quality and keeps well after harvesting. Its firm flesh offers a simple flavor. If you are one who tends to miss harvests, then this cultivar is for you, as the fruit is highly visible and obvious when ripe. Plant this one near your front door for its edible landscape appeal! (3% seed by weight)

Wabash

The "cannonball" of Peterson's selection, favored by many for its creamy, rich yellow-to-orange pulp and large size. The Wabash is a round, cannonball-shaped fruit with medium-firm texture. It is less common in the nursery industry, perhaps due to lower grafting percentages and slower timing to fruit production. That said, the fruit's quality makes this cultivar worth the effort. (6% seed by weight)

Tallahatchie

An exciting new release! The Tallahatchie was developed along with Neal's other selections, but was not released until 2019 because of his concern that the large clusters made harvest difficult. Pawpaw fruit that grow in a cluster do not ripen simultaneously; rather, over a period of days. Through constant urging by those savvy to the tree's qualities, this cultivar has finally been named and released.

This cultivar offers a pleasant aroma and sweet mellow flavor with floral notes and a silky smooth texture. Yields are medium to high, so fruit thinning may be needed. The fruit ripens mid- to late-season. In Maryland, for example, this would be mid-to-late September. The Tallahatchie has many appealing features:

- A pleasant aroma and sweet mellow flavor with floral notes and a silky smooth texture
- Medium to high yields
- Ripens mid- to late-season (in Maryland, for example, this would be mid-to-late September)
- The fruit averages 240 grams, or 9 ounces
- Contains few seeds, with the seed-to-fruit ratio at 5%

See the Resources appendix for licensed nurseries that carry Peterson Pawpaw selections and keep an eye out for future releases.

Kentucky State University

KSU has planted over 12 acres of pawpaw trees for genetic selection, commercial viability, and cultivar trialing since 1994. As of 2019, they have released three named cultivars: KSU-Atwood™, KSU-Benson™, and KSU-Chappell™.

KSU-Atwood™

KSU's Atwood is a great producer. This first KSU release was named after a former beloved university president. The Atwood was selected to help expand commercial qualities with consistently high yields, tasty fruit, and strong branching. The durable, right-angle branching of this cultivar is key for areas with strong winds, especially around harvest time when branches with heavy crop load can snap or drop fruits. The Atwood's skin turns greenish-blue when ripe, and its pulp is yellow or orange. This mild, tasty fruit blends hints of mango, pineapple, and banana and is a good all-around choice suited for a fresh market or pulping. Atwood has a moderate resistance to cracking issues, as well as the *Phyllosticta asminae* fungus that commonly attacks some pawpaws. The Atwood produces medium-sized fruits with an average of 150 fruits per tree!

KENTUCKY STATE UNIVERSITY PAWPAW RESEARCH PROGRAM

"Kentucky State University has the only full-time pawpaw research program in the world as part of the KSU Land Grant Program. Pawpaw research efforts are directed at improving propagation methods, developing orchard management recommendations, conducting regional variety trials, understanding fruit ripening and storage techniques, and germplasm collection and characterization of genetic diversity."

KSU-Benson™

The KSU-Benson was unveiled at the 4th International Pawpaw Conference at KSU in September 2016. This cultivar is a high-yielding release with medium- to large-sized round fruit boasting a thick, creamy texture, low seed-to-pulp ratio, and orange pulp with excellent flavor. The Benson is an early- to mid-season producer producing attractive round fruits that are well-suited for packing and shipping, adding to its appeal.

KSU-Chappell™

Vigorous growing, productive, and a very tasty selection—that is how I would describe the KSU-Chappell. KSU hit all the high notes on this one: very fruity with many tropical notes yielding to rich, complex flavor profiles; a thick, creamy texture; and large, healthy foliage to boot! Released in September 2018, the Chappell produces medium- to large-sized fruit and is reputed to be a very vigorous and strong grower. See Resources appendix for licensed nurseries that carry KSU selections and keep an eye out for future releases.

Jerry Lehman's Selections

Jerry Lehman was a bona fide pawpaw and persimmon culturist from Terre Haute, Indiana. His life's work with both the pawpaw and persimmon has been outstanding and award winning. It is safe to say that without Jerry Lehman, the fruit world would be much less diverse.

Jerry planted over 500 hand-bred pawpaw trees that are laid out in many rows on his property in Terre Haute. He tracked his trees by stating the row number as the distance from his property line and then the number down each row; i.e., 250-30. I would imagine that many of Jerry's selections will eventually be named cultivars and become more widely available in the nursery trade; for now, you have to have faith and plant these choice genetics.

Maria's Joy (166-13)

Maria's Joy is a controlled cross that marries the fruit qualities of Davis with the vigor of Prolific. This pawpaw is so good, it won the Best 1st Place at the 2012 Ohio Pawpaw Festival[9], and, reportedly, it is a favorite of visitors to Jerry's extensive orchard. Maria's Joy produces medium- to large-sized kidney-shaped fruit with yellow pulp. It is a consistent and heavy producer.

Lehman's Delight (275-48)

Winner of the Ohio Pawpaw Festival's Biggest Pawpaw contest in 2011, 2012, and 2018, and also Best 2nd Place in 2013 and 2014, Lehman's Delight produces large to very large fruit with excellent, very sweet flavor. It is a mid- to late-season producer.

THE BOTTOM LINE

There are a variety of cultivars available to the grower, depending on the type of fruit you desire.

Milder flavors:
- Shenandoah
- Mango
- Sue
- Overleese
- KSU-Atwood

For a challenging growing site:
- Sunflower
- Mango
- PA Golden
- KSU-Atwood

Richer, full flavor notes:
- Susquehanna
- PA Golden
- KSU-Chappell

Northern-reaching climates and cool summer areas:
- PA Golden
- Summer's Delight
- KSU-Benson
- NC-1
- Ford Amend

Extra ornamental benefits, plus fabulous fruits:
- NC-1
- Davis
- Rappahannock
- KSU-Atwood
- KSU-Chappell
- Susquehanna
- KSU-Chappell

For the biggest fruits:
- Potomac
- Lehman's Delight

If in doubt, stick with the long-proven cultivars of Overleese, Sunflower, PA Golden, and NC-1. T

---

9 The Best Pawpaw Competition is based on the following categories: weight, appearance, skin surface, aroma, skin thickness, front flavor, texture, aftertaste, and seeds.

CHAPTER 3

GROWING PAWPAWS FROM SEED AND GRAFTING

Pawpaws: the first year they sleep, the second year they creep,
and the third year they leap!

Pawpaws are very hardy and low maintenance plants if they are grown correctly.

Collecting and Storing Seed

The golden rule to growing a pawpaw tree from seed is to never let the seed dry out. So, when you have just finished the delightful experience of eating a pawpaw and you have decided to grow your own tree, place those seeds directly in the ground where you want to grow your tree. Not ready to grow your tree right away? You can put your seeds in a resealable plastic bag in the refrigerator[1]. Leaving your seeds in room-temperature conditions will cause them to dry out, killing the tiny embryo and prohibiting germination.

Be sure to clean all the flesh off the seeds before storing. If the seeds are coming from rotted fruit, give them a five-minute soak in a diluted solution of bleach: a 1:10 ratio of bleach to water is recommended. The seeds need a minimum of 70 to 100 days of chilling at temperatures slightly above freezing. This is known as "stratifying" the seed—a fancy word that means you are mimicking what happens naturally to

---

1 It is best to put the seeds into the refrigerator within the first 24 hours after cleaning. Sooner the better.

Image courtesy of Trevor Newman, known as The Fruit Nut, who is dedicated to exploring and popularizing uncommon and under-utilized fruiting plants. Check him out at www.thefruitnut.com.

temperate zone seeds when overwintering outside. Seeds not directly planted in the ground are typically chilled in the refrigerator between 32° and 40°F (or 0° to 4°C). Storing them longer than 100 days is fine since seeds collected during harvest season—late August through early October—often do not germinate until the following spring. For me, that could mean up to seven months in the refrigerator. Just keep an eye out that they do not begin to get moldy from being too damp.

Adding a damp medium, such as sand, to the bag can help maintain the needed moisture; however, if you have enough seeds in the bag, they need no extra medium. Be sure to poke a few needle-sized holes in the bag to vent excess moisture. I keep an eye on my seeds and simply rinse them if there is any fungal buildup.

A Pot is Not a Pot

A pot is not a pot, no it is not, not anymore! There are tall ones, short ones, skinny ones, fat ones, square ones, round ones, shallow ones, deep ones . . . What is one to do?

The one time you will catch me encouraging the "straight and narrow" is when it comes to growing pawpaws in pots. I am a big fan of growing pawpaws in deep (12+ inches) tree pots for a number of reasons: to accommodate the pawpaw's deep tap root; to achieve good moisture retention; to avoid spiraling of the tap root; and for ease of storing together. Given the right medium and space, germinating pawpaw seeds will send down a nine-inch tap root before shooting up a stem. Deep pots without large openings in the bottom hold moisture well, dramatically reducing frequency of watering and encouraging deep root growth. Straight, narrow sides guide the growing roots downward, preventing the roots from circling and becoming root bound. Tall, rectangular pots fit beautifully together in milk crates, making storage and transportation more efficient.

Popular in the nursery trade are root trainer pots, also known as air-pruning pots. Rectangular in shape, these pots encourage roots to grow down and out through large holes in the bottom where the dry air kills the growing tips. When the air prunes the bottom roots, more lateral roots are encouraged to grow, thus building up more root mass. The down side to this design is that it requires a mesh-bottomed surface to hold the pots a few feet above the ground, necessitating the need for more watering. They work, but they take work.

Watering plants in pots takes real dedication, one that life does not always accommodate. I like to design for neglect or low inputs when considering watering needs. The deep tree pots allow moisture to linger much longer than shallow pots and certainly longer than the popular air-pruned pots. I find that deep pots and balanced shade (30-50%) allows me to minimize watering needs for my potted pawpaws and many other nursery plants.

Note there are also creative reuse options, such as fashioning deep tree tubes from old tree shelters and tall milk cartons.

My niece, Ruby Rasmey Judd, standing in front of a pawpaw tree at Long Creek Homestead holding a milk crate full of 1-year-old pawpaw saplings in 12-inch-deep pots.

Germinating Seeds – Roots to Shoots

Pawpaws are slow to start but easy to grow.

The saying with pawpaws is that the first year they sleep, the second year they creep, and the third year they leap! With pawpaw trees, it's all about getting the roots well established. The motto to remember is "roots to shoots." Pawpaws seeds have high germination rates (over 90%) when a couple of key elements and a single virtue are considered. The elements are temperature and moisture. The virtue is patience.

Pawpaw seed sprouting its root!

ROBBING PETER TO PAY PAUL: POTTING MIXES

Peat moss, vermiculite, perlite, and coconut coir all make great potting mixes; however, the environmental impact of these options does not justify the benefits. Peat and sphagnum mosses come from rich ecosystems that get drained, dug out, and shipped afar. Vermiculite and perlite also come from afar after they get blasted with energy-intensive high heat to cause expansion. While coconut coir—the pith from coconuts—often is an environmentally championed alternative that acts like a peat replacement, it, too, has a big footprint on the ecologies and people processing it half a world away. Using these products basically means you are robbing one ecosystem to build up another.

To make your own eco-groovy soil mix, you can buy the individual ingredients and mix them yourself or make your own from scratch. I recommend making a potting mix using a recipe of two parts sieved compost, two parts good topsoil, two parts composted tree bark or wood chips, and one part worm castings. Aged sawdust, if available, is also a good add, but must be rotted or else it robs nitrogen from the soil mix. I make my soil mix heavier than traditional mixes by adding more top soil than most, as I find it adds natural fertility and moisture-holding properties. This means I have to feed and water less.

Potting mixes ideally have healthy fungal networks and natural fertility

Regardless of your germination technique, consistent moisture is key. Pawpaw seeds should never dry out. How long it takes for your pawpaw seeds to germinate is determined by temperature.

Direct Seeding

If you direct seed in the autumn by taking the seed from a freshly eaten pawpaw and planting it where you'd like it to grow—known as "direct seeding"—germination will begin the following summer. The seeds will cold stratify naturally over the winter in the ground and then slowly begin to germinate as the soils warm again, usually revealing a growing shoot in July or August.

While direct seeding is a long affair that requires care to assure good and consistent moisture, it has the benefit of avoiding transplanting, which pawpaws certainly appreciate. For direct seeding, prepare your planting site by creating a well-draining topsoil two to four inches deep. Sow your seeds flat with approximately one inch of soil above the seed. Mulch well with straw or other mulch material to ensure good moisture retention and protect against extended hard freezes. Ideally, at this time you would mulch an extensive area to start the soil conditioning for the tree's future growth (see Planned Planting section in Chapter 4). Placing a piece of chicken wire or hardware cloth over the soil before mulching will help block curious rodents; just be sure to remove the protective covering before sprouting takes place the following summer. Young seedlings sown or planted in direct sunlight prefer shade for the first year or two, so create a shade structure or put in place a short (18") tree tube.

GUERILLA ACTION

Pawpaws readily grow from seed, as proven by the many pawpaw seedlings we have popping up all over our homestead—a result of raccoon feastings. While raccoons are the ultimate guerilla planters, we humans can also guerilla plant pawpaws in vacant areas. Consider making pawpaw seed bombs by encasing the seeds in balls of absorbent material, such as clay and compost, and tossing them into neglected areas such as urban waste lands, park edges, or your neighbor's yard. Or even easier: just throw a whole pawpaw fruit into those areas!

Slow but Sure Method

Seed germinating time can be sped up by starting seeds inside your home or any heated space. After you have stratified seeds in the refrigerator, place the seeds directly in deep pots using a moist potting mix that has been warmed to room temperature (75° to 85°F or 24° to 29°C) in your home or greenhouse. Insert the seeds, flat side down, with one inch of soil covering the seed. Maintain consistent moisture in the pots. I help maintain moisture in my pots during early-stage germination by mini-mulching with woodchips or sand on the surface. I also keep them in the dark (pawpaw seeds do not need light to begin the germination process)—this allows slow moisture evaporation and does not use up precious

1. The seed imbibes water.
2. The radicle splits the seed coat and emerges.
3. Root development occurs.
4. The green growing tip emerges above soil and expands its leaves.

light space in the house. At room temperature, initial root emergence is approximately one month; after that, it takes approximately six to eight weeks for the first shoots to begin emerging. When the shoot emerges, it is hypogeal, meaning the seed leaves (cotyledons) remain below the soil surface and the first leaves of the emerging shoot are true leaves. At this stage, be sure the plants have indirect light and warmth. While it is best to keep the pots inside (giving the plants a consistently warm temperature, thus increasing growth rates), if it is past the freezing date outdoors, plants can be moved outside to the shade of a deciduous tree or beneath a shade cloth in full sun. If you use shade cloth in full sun, 30-50% shade cloth is recommended.

Remember the mantra with starting pawpaws: patience, patience, patience—and consistent moisture.

Wyatt Judd showing off our simple, yet abundant, germination set up

The Deluxe Germination Method

To gain a couple of weeks in the germination game, I use a small heating mat that controls the temperature of my soil medium and causes my seeds to germinate the root tip in just 14 days. This is the fastest process I know of. Using this technique, my germination rates have been in the 90% range.

I received this germination method from pawpaw grower legend Jim Davis of Deep Run Pawpaw Orchard. Using just a single heating mat to heat the soil, a pair of turkey basting pans, and a lightweight seeding mix, seeds will begin germination in just 14 days. Now, I germinate hundreds of seeds at a time for my nursery business; the same method works well for even just a handful of seeds.

Be sure your mat has an adjustable thermostat and set it at 85°F.[2] Place an empty aluminum pan on the mat, moisten the seedling mix, and layer it one-inch thick in the pan. Place pawpaw seeds flat, side by side, and cover the seeds with an additional one inch of moistened potting mix. Repeat up to three layers if you have enough seed. Regardless of having one or three layers, make sure the seeds have an

---

2 The best heating mats have a small metal probe that are inserted into the potting medium to measure the actual temperature (versus the temperature of the mat heat). I often have to turn my mat up to 87°F or more to maintain the desired 85°F in the potting medium.

inch of seedling mix below and above them; think of it as pawpaw-seed lasagna! Cover your lasagna with an upside-down pan as the lid, and clamp together the two pans. Check every couple of days to be sure the potting medium stays moist. Seed coats will split in approximately 14 days; you will see the white root tip showing. Pick them out as soon as the root pokes out, then pot them with the root radical facing down in deep pots or directly in the ground where they will be grown. Note that placing a piece of insulation, such as folded cardboard, under the heating mat helps keep the heat from sinking into the surface below.

Squirrels and Chipmunks

Beware that curious squirrels and chipmunks like to root into pots in search of food and to bury their nuts; this can destroy your young pawpaw seedlings. Historically, I have lost upwards of a third of my nursery stock to such diggings; now I grow them in critter-proof A-frame structures covered in chicken wire. This method also conveniently supports the use of a shade cloth. An unused chicken coop or chicken tractor can be easily retrofitted into a pawpaw nursery. I have also reused an A-framed children's play set as a ready-made nursery.

I converted an old A-frame chicken coop into my pawpaw nursery by simply placing 50% shade cloth over the chicken wire. This is in full sun, but does not need constant watering thanks to the shade cloth and deep pots. It is safe from deer and nut-burying squirrels. As an eventual replacement for the shade cloth, I have planted honey locust trees around the coop that, once grown, will give perfectly dappled shade.

Timing

I begin germinating my pawpaw seeds in Maryland, which is located in USDA zone 6b, around mid-February using the deluxe method. I transplant the germinating seeds into pots in early March, allow the tap root to develop for six to eight weeks, and then place them outside under the shade cloth or under a tree in late April/early May when the shoots are emerging, the weather is warming, and the danger of a hard frost has passed.

I plant the small pawpaw seedlings that have sprouted in March in autumn of that same year when the leaves begin to change color; sometimes, I wait until the following spring. Doing this reduces the risk of the tap root outgrowing the tree pots. The pawpaw tap root, like most nut trees, is ready to shoot deep into the earth—not hang out in a pot. The seedling root will reach the bottom of a 12-inch-deep tree pot in just six months! Planting in early or mid-autumn[3] reduces the concern about over-wintering potted pawpaws, which need protection from freezing. Those that I do over-winterize, I put in an unheated garage or in straw bale forts that buffer against hard freezes.

TRUE TO HEREDITY

"True to heredity" is a horticultural term meaning a plant that is grown from seed will be like its "parents." Some fruit seeds, including pawpaws, have good genetic overlap; that is, they will likely have good fruit quality if their parents did. This is a good attribute when seeds are collected in a cultivated pawpaw orchard, as the plants grown from these seeds will have many of the high qualities of their parents. That said, seeds from cultivated pawpaws will not have the same guarantee of production and quality as a grafted cultivar.

If the pawpaws you have been eating and saving seed from are superior cultivars, then those seeds, quite possibly, will grow and produce a decent fruit without needing to graft a named cultivar onto it. In the nursery trade, these are called "select pawpaw seedlings." They are not named cultivars, even though they may be seed from, say, the famed Shenandoah cultivar, but they will have a mix of the parents' genetics. Select seedlings are fine for home-scale growing, but not always recommended for market production where the assurance of 100% quality that comes from grafted cultivars is a wise investment. Not to mention that it takes a seedling six or seven years to reach maturity and produce fruit, whereas a grafted plant takes only four or five years to fruit.

Collecting and growing out wild pawpaw seeds is a fine idea if you plan to graft them later; otherwise, you are rolling the dice on fruit quality. See the Resources appendix for quality seed suppliers.

---

3 Planting in early to mid-autumn is ideal. Avoid planting in late autumn when winter is near.

This quick planting of seedling trees is ideal. Planting pawpaw trees at two years of age or older works too; however, it will incur more maintenance and careful care of the tree while residing in a pot to reduce the risk of stunting. Planting a pawpaw tree that is three years or older increases the occurrence of long-term health and productivity issues due to root restriction and damage. The effects of restricted roots in pots will likely not be prevalent for many years and not blatantly obvious to one who is not keenly observing, which is why many will say "bah" to this insistence of the tap root care and claim that trees from cramped pots will do just fine. Maybe I am just being a pawpaw tap root fanatic . . . or maybe I am focusing on where the pawpaw energy naturally wants to grow.

If I intend to graft the planted pawpaw trees, I will "site graft" them where they are planted in the spring of the second or third year of their life, or grow them in 14+-inch-deep tree pots for grafting and resale.

Grafting Pawpaws

Pawpaws graft easily. If you have never grafted anything, please do not be put off on trying since it is fun and not super complicated—especially with pawpaws.

What is Grafting?

Grafting is a union of two plants, where one plant is selected for its roots—this is called the rootstock—and another plant is selected for its quality of fruits, which is called the scion or budwood. The rootstock

offers strong growing characteristics and resistance to harsh conditions, while the scion is a guarantee of desired genetics (fruit quality). When these two are successfully joined together, you get the best of both worlds.

Scion wood is a cutting taken from the previous year's growth from a plant known for high-quality fruit; once grafted onto the rootstock, it will produce the same high-quality fruit. The scion is an exact genetic clone to the tree it came from.

Rootstock plants are hardy plants, usually grown from seed, which are known to have strong growth characteristics and adaptability to local conditions. They often do not have a guarantee of high-quality fruit.

All variations of grafting are about lining up the cambium layers—the thin layer of actively growing cells between the wood and bark—on the rootstock and scion wood. When the cambium layers are matched up, joined smoothly, and kept from drying out, they heal together and the vascular systems unite. Thus, the graft becomes one functioning plant!

Grafting does not take specialized skill—rather, practice! I teach grafting workshops to first-time growers who, after just an hour of explanation and practice, can successfully graft a young fruit tree. It is not as tricky as one might think. Like most growing, it takes timing, quality materials, and attention to detail. If you can drive a car or use a computer, you can graft a fruit tree.

Another way to describe grafting is that it is a form of asexual propagation, especially used when a plant is incapable of forming roots on its cuttings. This is the case with pawpaw trees, as they are incapable of rooting cuttings, even with hormone treatment.

Why Graft?

Many plants do not come true from seed. For example, seed taken from a "Sunflower" pawpaw fruit will grow a pawpaw tree, but it will not be a Sunflower cultivar; rather, it will be a mix of two parents.

WHAT IS THE BEST ROOTSTOCK?

There is no agreement among growers for what is the best rootstock choice for pawpaws. Seeds grown out from the popular Sunflower are touted quite a bit, as it is a vigorous and strong grower. Many people also hold to using seeds from regional wild trees for growing out rootstock. The simple answer is that seed from any healthy-growing pawpaw tree can be grown out and grafted onto; this is the norm in the nursery industry.

Food for thought, however, has come from conversations with Jim Davis of Deep Run Pawpaw Orchard. Jim has been growing around 1,000 pawpaw trees for over 20 years, all the while making keen observations. He points out that rootstock, with strong hybrid vigor, such as seedlings grown out from Sunflower, potentially have higher management demands, at least in productive orchards.

Pruning is a key piece of highly productive pawpaw trees, and strong-growing rootstock can add to the maintenance of keeping trees balanced for air flow and ease of harvest. A second piece to consider with grafted cultivars on vigorous rootstock is the potential for overbearing. The added workload required to thin fruit—which sounds like a good challenge to have, but on a larger scale or for those who don't keep up with thinning—is not a bonus.

That said, Jim has one row in his extensive orchard that has grafted trees on rootstock that came from locally gathered wild pawpaw seed. He has noted in years of drought stress that this row is notably greener and more resistant than the rest of the orchard, which has a mix of hybrid seedling as rootstock. Jim's observation makes a strong statement for using regionally gathered seed from wild pawpaw stands for naturally built-in resilience.

To assure a replica of the Sunflower's qualities, a branch end with buds—i.e., scion wood—needs to be grafted onto a pawpaw seedling—i.e., the rootstock. Once the graft takes hold, meaning it melds together into one plant, the scion becomes the entire upper portion of the tree, while the rootstock remains the root system and will become the first foot or so of the trunk. Since the scion is basically a clone cutting, the tree will produce the exact same genetics as the Sunflower and will be a Sunflower cultivar. Grafting can also speed up the number of years it takes the tree to become fruit bearing; typically, grafting will yield fruit at least one to two years earlier than trees grown from seed.

Collecting and Storing Scion

Scion wood is noticeable by its lighter color and ranges in length from three inches to three feet, depending on the tree's growth rate. For springtime grafting, the scion is collected in late winter while still dormant. Ideally, it is harvested as part of annual pruning. Look for healthy branch ends approximately ¼- to ⅜-inch in diameter, with plump buds. Cut scions about 8 to 10 inches long—or as long as possible— then label and store in resealable plastic bags with a damp paper towel. Place scions in the refrigerator until late spring when it is time to graft. Keep an eye out for mold growth on the paper towel and replace if necessary.

When selecting pawpaw scion wood, you will see a mix of vegetative leaf buds (long and pointed) and possibly fuzzy brown flower buds. If your scion has fuzzy flower buds, keep them attached while storing. Ideally, scion wood is collected from trees that have already reached an age of fruiting. Scion from trees too young to have borne fruit may take longer to begin fruiting once grafted.

When cutting scion wood for storage, do so just above a bud at an angle to help it heal cleanly. Though not always necessary, I cover the cut ends of scions with a little beeswax or paraffin wax to help seal in moisture for storage. Keeping the scion wood moist in the refrigerator is key to it staying viable for the two to three months before grafting onto the rootstock. Remember to label the scions with the cultivar or select tree name!

Types of Grafts

One of the reasons grafting inhibits newbies from jumping in is the myriad of different types and names of grafts. Once you understand that the differently named grafts are essentially variations of the same procedure, much confusion will drop away. Choosing a graft style is

Neal Peterson visiting us one late winter to gather scion wood for his international distribution

This picture of a pawpaw branch tip by uncommon fruit guru Lee Reich shows clear demarcation of color change of the scion wood and dormant flower buds

largely based on personal preference and size of the rootstock. Here I will discuss the cleft graft; it is my favorite for grafting pawpaw seedlings and I find it to be the easiest for beginners.

When to Graft?

Pawpaw seedlings are commonly grafted when the plant stems are about pencil thickness, in late spring when leaves are an inch or so long, or later in the summer for budding. Grafting scion wood in late spring is the easiest method for novice grafters.

For successful results when grafting, pawpaws need to be in an active-growth stage, which, for scion wood grafting, is soon after the first leaves of the season emerge. At this stage, the nutrients and sap are flowing, which allows the graft union to quickly meld together, healing and growing as one plant. If growth has been strong, seedling pawpaw trees can be grafted at just one year of age; however, they typically are grafted in their second or third year once they achieve pencil thickness. Ideally, the scion and rootstock are close to the same diameter. They can be grafted in pots or where they are growing in the ground.

Consistent temperatures above 55°F both day and night increase grafting success. If you are grafting in pots, the ideal is to keep them inside once grafted, where temperatures and light levels are steady. Once the graft heals together, and outside temperatures are consistently above 55°F around the clock, gradually move the newly grafted trees to a protected shady location outside. It is not recommended with pawpaws to graft and plant in the same season. If you graft a potted pawpaw tree in the spring, wait until autumn of that year or spring of the following year to plant, as pawpaw trees need recovery time from transplanting. This goes for bare-root plantings of pawpaws as well; wait a season or a year after planting to graft.

Tools and Materials

Having the latest and grooviest grafting supplies certainly makes the process go easy, but by no means is it necessary. I learned grafting in rural Nicaragua using mango and avocado trees. The only tool I had was a honed-down hacksaw blade fashioned into a bamboo handle and plastic bags with which to wrap the grafts. Believe it or not, this worked great!

I will describe a more modern grafting method than the way I learned. The trick is to keep your scion wood in good condition and make sure the graft never dries out. To begin, you will need the following:

- Thin, sharp blade, such as a Swiss army knife, utility knife, or grafting knife. It is important for the blade to be sharp and stay sharp. After all, this is surgery you are performing—tree surgery! Grafting knives are preferred, but others will do if sharp. Note that specialty grafting knives come in left-hand and right-hand options; only one side of the blade is sharpened, which helps to make long, smooth cuts.
- Parafilm grafting tape.[4] Grafting tape sticks to itself and decomposes naturally, which avoids potential girdling of the graft union. Other elastic tapes, rubber bands, and electricians' tape can work, as long as care is given to monitor and remove it once the graft has taken hold to avoid girdling.
- Beeswax or paraffin wax can be used as additional insurance against moisture loss.
- Grafting tools that make exact cuts on both the scion and rootstock are optional, as good grafting tools can be expensive.

PAW PAW SEEDLING CLEFT GRAFT

KEEP 2-3 BUDS

SCIONWOOD

6"

ROOTSTOCK

CUT ROOTSTOCK AND SCIONWOOD

SLOWLY SLIDE SCION INTO ROOTSTOCK

LINE UP CAMBIUM LAYERS

WRAP WITH PARAFILM TAPE

OPTIONAL: COVER WITH MELTED BEESWAX

4 Not all grafting tape is made equal. Many are cheap, don't stretch well, and break easily. My preferred grafting tape is Buddy Tape. See Resources for supplier.

The Cleft Graft

When the saplings begin to leaf out—for pawpaws, this is later than most other trees (around early May for those of us in Maryland)—it is time to graft on the stored scions[5]. The following outline is for potted plants or seedling trees that have been in the ground for at least one year.

With the cleft graft, the rootstock seedling is cut off completely about six inches above the soil, or where the thickness best matches the scion, using a clean straight cut with sharp pruning shears. It is okay if the rootstock diameter is larger than the scion, but not okay if the scion is larger than the rootstock. The perfect—yet tricky—scenario is for both the scion and rootstock to be the same diameter.

Cut your scion to two or three leaf buds. Longer pieces of scion have a tendency to dry out while healing together with the rootstock. If the scion is filled with flower buds that look like small, furry balls, remove them so that the adjacent dormant vegetative bud can sprout. Make the cut to the scion just above a bud so there is a smooth section of wood to work. The base of the scion is then sliced with opposing cuts to form a long, V-shaped wedge. Try to make one long, smooth cut about half an inch long on each side of the scion by starting at the base of the blade then moving out to the tip in a single, sweeping cut. A smooth cut allows the cambium to "kiss" tightly with the corresponding cambium in the rootstock. If need be, keep whittling the cuts until smooth and no light shows between the scion and rootstock when fitted together. Try not to touch the cut area with your fingers, as it may infect the surgery; however, it is okay to place the cut scion in your mouth while prepping the rootstock.

Now, on the rootstock that has been cut off flush, make a vertical slit down the center about the depth of the knife, moving carefully and using controlled pressure so you don't split the stem too deep. Slide the V-shaped scion down into the rootstock slit, slowly and carefully. If the scion and the rootstock are of different diameter, which they often are, be sure to line up one side of the scion cambium to the root-stock cambium; don't worry about the other side lining up. Tightly wrap the union with grafting tape or other type of band, being sure to overlap the cut portions generously. The key here is to keep the union from drying out. With good grafting tape, you can cover the entire scion, buds included, to help maintain moisture (just try to keep the tape to one layer over the buds to allow the buds to be able to push through the tape). Alternatively, after wrapping the union, the entire scion can be covered with a soft wax (such as beeswax or paraffin wax) to help assure it doesn't dry out.

Once grafted, keep well-watered, safe from freezing weather, and out of full sunlight. Usually, you will see the scion buds pushing new growth within two to three weeks. If the graft does not take, the scion will dry up and the rootstock will usually re-sprout below the graft, at which point you can wait another year to try grafting again or try chip bud grafting in the summer.[6]

---

5 If you have a greenhouse, your trees may wake up and begin blooming earlier. If so, grafting can take place in early spring.
6 Sheri Crabtree of Kentucky State University has a good YouTube video of chip budding pawpaw trees. Simply search "Pawpaw: chip-budding trees."

Watch for any shoots sprouting below the scion on the rootstock and pinch them off to keep the energy flowing to the scion. Even after years in the ground, keep an eye out for shoots arising from the rootstock base. Many people let this observation go and before long cannot tell what is the grafted part! This also goes for suckers coming off the roots: keep them cut down, lest your grafted tree will be stuck in the middle of a patch.

I typically plant out my successful grafts in pots the same autumn or the following spring. Alternatively, seedlings can be planted directly where they are to be grown and, once established, grafted in place. This is known as site or field grafting and has worked well for me. For site grafting, I also use the cleft graft process.

Top-Grafting

Top-grafting or top-working refers to grafting scions onto mature trees. This is sometimes called "reworking" if swapping out a previous cultivar. If you have mature, wild pawpaw trees with poor fruit quality or a cultivar you do not like, they can be cut back and grafted onto. Top-grafting is most successful on healthy trees that will be able to take the hard cutting back necessary for this type of grafting. Old trees are not good candidates. Ideally, trees to be top-grafted are less than five inches in diameter.

Many people have well-established pawpaw trees growing wild on their property that have poor-quality fruit. If the trees are receiving partial or full sun, then top-grafting them is a good idea in order to yield high-quality fruit.

There are multiple grafting techniques for top-grafting; however, for simplicity sake, we will stick with the cleft graft. When top-grafting a rootstock that is large in diameter, you can insert one or two scions. Inserting two scions increases your chances for success; however, if both are successful, remove one as you only need one graft.

Get started by giving the mature rootstock tree a boost. Clear at least a 10-foot diameter around the tree and mulch well. Once the tree's leaves emerge in spring, retrieve your scion from the refrigerator. Use a sharp pruning saw to cut back the tree on a slight angle below its existing branches, one to three feet from the ground. Cut the scion wood to two or three buds, then make opposing cuts at the bottom end to form a V-wedge. Using a large knife, split the top of the rootstock down the middle and hold it open. Insert your scion wood on either side, being sure to line up the cambium on the outside edges. Cover the entire area and scion wood with grafting wax. Alternatively, you can use parafilm tape over the entire area, optionally adding a layer of wax, as well. See the Resources appendix for more information on grafting.

CHAPTER 4

PAWPAW PLANTING 101

The ideal planting time for pawpaws occurs twice a year: in mid-spring, following any chance of freezing temperatures, and early- to mid-autumn, when the ground is still warm and air temperatures remain mild.

When to Plant

When pawpaw trees are planted is as important as *how* they are planted. There are ideal planting windows for best pawpaw tree establishment. The sweet spots for planting are late autumn and mid-spring. Avoid planting in the heat of summer or dead of winter.

I plant my deep-potted pawpaw trees while they are dormant[1] or newly leafing out and the weather is cool; this allows a smooth transition with minimal transplant shock. In Maryland where we live— USDA zones 6/7—my windows for planting typically are in April and May and again in late September and October. Autumn plantings before leaf fall have the added benefits of being planted into soils already warmed by summer temperatures, allowing some root growth to begin even when leaves have fallen from the trees. This bit of added root growth helps trees establish better for the next growing season and reduces watering needs the following summer. Planting later toward the winter season can cause failure as pawpaw roots go dormant when temperatures turn colder and root damage caused during transplantation cannot be repaired. Planting in early summer, due to the higher temperatures, stresses leafed-out plants and can also lead to failure.

---

1 Pawpaw trees are late to break dormancy and leaf out. This is a protective measure developed over eons to help guard against late frost. A similar phenomenon occurs in black walnut and American persimmon trees.

PLANTING: PLANNED VERSUS IMPROMPTU

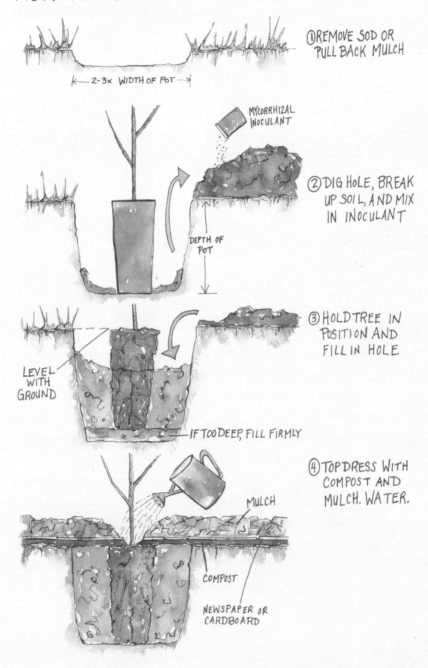

HOW TO PLANT A PAWPAW TREE

① REMOVE SOD OR PULL BACK MULCH

2-3x WIDTH OF POT

MYCORRHIZAL INOCULANT

② DIG HOLE, BREAK UP SOIL, AND MIX IN INOCULANT

DEPTH OF POT

③ HOLD TREE IN POSITION AND FILL IN HOLE

LEVEL WITH GROUND

IF TOO DEEP, FILL FIRMLY

④ TOP DRESS WITH COMPOST AND MULCH. WATER.

MULCH

COMPOST

NEWSPAPER OR CARDBOARD

The Importance of Shade

Young pawpaw trees, especially seedlings, that are planted in full sun will need a shade structure for the first year or two[2] because top growth on pawpaw trees is slow for the first couple of years as the plant puts its energy into developing a strong, deep taproot. At year three, or when the tree has grown to 18" or taller, no shading is needed. Once the young trees are established in full sun and good site conditions, the root systems will pump water and nutrients upward to support top growth of about a foot or more each year.

There are multiple creative ways to rig this early shade structure. I have tried the following:

An Oesco tree guard provides both shade and ventilation to a young pawpaw tree.

- Short tree tubes work okay if they have really good ventilation and are wide enough; otherwise, tubes can create funky conditions that make the young trees struggle.
- Custom-made welded wire fences 24" tall with 50% shade cloth "caps" work well for ventilation, just be sure the cloth hangs over sufficiently. A tomato cage would also work well.
- Oesco, Inc. makes a heavy-duty black polyethylene tree guard that joins the best of shade and ventilation. Typically, I do not like buying fabricated materials; however, this is a perfect product for establishing multiple pawpaw seedlings. It is only available in 100-foot-long rolls, so it is not a great investment for the home grower with just a handful of trees.

Planned Planting

The ideal pawpaw tree planting site would be prepared a year or more in advance, especially if poor soils exist. Planned planting is basically composting and mulching the planting site to allow nature to begin the soil-conditioning process. Time spent upfront conditioning soil will pay off in successful transplanting and strong plant growth.

---

2   Many growers are observing that if young pawpaw trees have adequate moisture and good mulching, then shade structures are not needed past the first year. To be safe, two years is recommended for novice growers.

TRANSPLANTING SUCKERS

Pawpaw trees will send out horizontal roots that send up "suckers" into what seems like a new tree, but is actually just a clone of the mother tree that is still intimately attached, like an umbilical cord.

Suckers can be successfully transplanted if separated carefully at the right time. Use a shovel to cut the connecting root to the mother plant on either side of the sucker up to one year before and no less than two weeks prior to the planned separation. Root severing before digging up allows the separation shock to wear off and new independent roots to begin forming. Then, either directly transplant it in a very well-prepared spot outdoors or pot it up. Either way, the transplant should be placed in the shade for the first year or two and closely monitored for water needs. The best time to dig up a sucker is early spring, before bud swell has occurred.

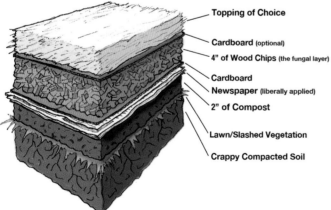

Mike's Deluxe Sheet Mulch

- Topping of Choice
- Cardboard (optional)
- 4" of Wood Chips (the fungal layer)
- Cardboard
- Newspaper (liberally applied)
- 2" of Compost
- Lawn/Slashed Vegetation
- Crappy Compacted Soil

There are many mulch recipes for preparing a planting site, ranging from layered manures and composts to simply plain wood chips. If time and resources allow, creating a "sheet mulch" gives the planting site a great head start. Sheet mulch is a permaculture term and is similar to "lasagna gardening," where multiple layers are placed directly on the ground in order to smother the sod, adding fertility and the ability to hold moisture.

The diagram from my book, *Edible Landscaping with a Permaculture Twist*[3], shows a layered approach that starts with compost and/or manure, followed by newspaper, woodchips, cardboard, and straw. This approach jump-starts years of soil-building in one go: the compost layer provides instant food for soil life to start munching, the newspaper helps kill off the sod while attracting worms, the wood chips draw in fungi, the cardboard traps moisture for the chips to attract fungi, and the straw caps it all off for optimal moisture protection. During the first growing season, the soil biota will consume the compost and much of the paper. Then the woodchips drop down, which degrade with the aid of fungi, and the soil biota continue to be fed and protected through the second and third year. After a year, pull back the composting layers in the center and dig out a planting hole. Be careful not to let the organic matter that has not yet decomposed mix back into the planting hole. Once planted, the decomposing mulch materials can be brought back around the tree, leaving a quarter- to half-inch of open space

3 To learn more about *Edible Landscaping with a Permaculture Twist,* visit www.ecologiadesign.com.

around the stem. Placing a ring of hardware cloth around the tree base helps hold mulch back at the perfect distance. This is also a good time to establish companion plants and ground covers.

A bare minimum site prep is to simply add a layer of cardboard with a 4" or deeper layer of hardwood chips to the planting area one year or more in advance of planting. The cardboard, combined with the wood chips, will kill off the sod and begin holding moisture for the soil below, which in turn will stimulate healthy soil life. Wood chips will draw in fungi that start breaking down the woody material into available nutrients and soil-building organic matter. By covering the wood chips with straw or other organic matter, you will speed up the decomposition process by trapping moisture, which fungi need to thrive.

Impromptu Planting

Impromptu plantings are just that: planting a tree with no previous site preparation into a sea of grass or weeds, or a combo of both, and typically in poor soil. Though impromptu plantings are not recommended, the reality is that it happens.

Thoughtful planting is critical to survival and establishment, with the keys to successful plantings being timing and the health of the tree being planted. Ideally, trees are planted when the weather is cool. This greatly reduces transplant stress, producing a tree with healthy roots that have not been compromised. Healthy trees planted at the right time largely make up for not having a previously prepared planting site.

There is an old saying, "Dig a $20.00 hole for a $5.00 tree," meaning one should dig a sufficiently deep and generously wide hole for the transplant, much larger than the root ball. Dig the hole the full depth of the potted tree and two to three times the width of the container or root ball. Digging a wide hole helps loosen the soil around the newly planted tree, allowing the roots to easily begin to spread out. Small tight holes can encourage the roots to wrap around within the limited space. Planting in soil that is wet from recent rains is not recommended. Wait until the soil crumbles, otherwise you risk changing the soil structure and creating compaction.

Here are some easy steps to follow:

1. Dig out the sod layer and shake all the soil loose.
2. Place the vegetative material to the side and continue digging and mounding the soil next to the hole. Be mindful that the dug-up soil that is spread out makes replanting it a real pain. I like to place a piece of cardboard or plywood next to the hole I am about to dig to help keep the dug-up soil clean and easy to return around the tree roots.
3. Discard any rocks.
4. Before removing the tree from the pot, test the depth with the tree still in the pot to be sure it will be even with the surrounding ground level. If you have dug too deep, replace some of the

A FEW PLANTING NOTES

If you are planting a bareroot plant, keep it covered and in a bucket of water with the roots fully submerged while you prep the planting hole. This keeps the roots hydrated and avoids damage from sun and wind.

Do not force roots into a shallow hole. If you hit a large rock that is not coming out, this is not a good place to plant the tree as pawpaws have deep tap roots. Choose a different spot to plant.

If your hole fills with water that sits for more than a couple of hours, it is not a good place for pawpaw trees to be planted, as they need soil that drains well.

I do not add any amendments to my dug soil other than a mycorrhizal inoculant*. By adding compost or other materials to the planting soil, you risk changing the planting hole's consistency compared to the surrounding soil. This can create a water-pooling effect in clay soils and encourage roots to stay wound in the amended area rather than venture out. I recommend top-down dressing the hole with compost and amendments that slowly get pulled down into the native soil, which gradually improves soil conditions. (See more about top-down dressing on the following page.)

*Note: A mycorrhizal inoculant can be made by collecting a handful of organic rich soil from the woods. If preferred, you can purchase an inoculant powder (see Resources). Simply mix your local forest matter or purchased inoculant with the ground soil as you plant.

soil and firm it to give the tap root an easier start. The danger in digging the hole too deep and replacing soil is that it can slump down with time and lower the tree into a depression. Just be sure to press firmly any soil added back in place.

5. Break up any soil clods. You want a fine, crumbly soil to place back around the roots. Have the soil returning into the hole readily prepared before removing the tree from the pot.

For potted pawpaw trees growing in deep pots, there is a bit of an art to successful potted-tree removal. I hold my pots upside down with my fingers spread out over the opening; with the tree stem between my fingers, I give a quick jerk. This releases the soil and roots all together. I then carefully turn it back over and place it directly into the hole. Alternatively, you can cut the pot off from around the soil. Either way, be sure to take your time during the removal process, as this will affect your transplant's success. If the tree does not come out well and you end up with a bare root plant, which occasionally happens, hold the plant in the hole so that roots are suspended at the correct depth and begin to slowly fill in your soil, being sure to firm the soil snuggly around the roots to avoid leaving air pockets. Having two people during this process is ideal so that one person can hold the tree at the correct height while the other focuses on slowly and carefully adding the soil around the roots. Be sure the pawpaw tree is planted at the same soil level height it was in the pot; for bare root trees, place the plant in the hole where the stem meets the root crown. Planting too deep or too shallow increases the chance of failure.

Once planted, you can add compost and other organic supplement to the surface; this is called top-down dressing. The nutrients and organic matter placed around the surface will gradually make their way down to the root zone without dramatically changing the hole's constitution. Be sure not to mound any organic matter against the stem as doing so can cause the stem to rot. Ideally, leave a quarter- to half-inch of breathing space around the stem. Learn more on feeding in Chapter 5: Eco-Logical Tree Care.

Fungi-rich soil after a few seasons of sheet mulching

Water your recently planted trees deeply to help settle the tree and eliminate any air pockets left from planting. While heavy mulching greatly reduces or relieves the need to water, it still may be required during times of high heat and drought. If a week passes without an inch of rain and the weather is hot, check the planting site by sticking your finger into the soil up to its first joint. If you feel moisture, do not water. Repeat the test every couple of days if it still has not rained. Only water when the soil feels dry, then do so thoroughly to encourage the roots to grow deep. With heavy sheet mulching (see "Planned Planting" above), combined with the humid Mid-Atlantic temperatures where we live in Maryland, watering beyond the planting stage is rare. Once established, pawpaw trees are moderately drought-tolerant thanks to the deep tap root.

Sheet Mulching with Impromptu Planting

If you go for the impromptu planting, you can retrofit the sheet mulch around the plant, and though the fertility benefits will take a season to kick in, you will have good moisture retention and weed suppression in place. See Appendix I: Pawpaws and Permaculture to explore more detail about planned planting techniques and companion planting.

A Quick Note on Deer

Typically, deer do not like eating pawpaw trees because of their chemical composition and foul taste. That said, in some areas, deer will nibble young plants, potentially killing the plant in the seedling stage. Seedling shade structures help protect the trees from early-growth browsing. Once well established—after three or four years—pawpaws can handle light browsing, even though it is not typical at this stage of growth. We have herds of deer that move through our homestead, and except for the occasional buck rubbing his antlers (known as "buck rub") on the trunk, they leave our mature pawpaws alone. Buck rub can be a big problem and cause of death or disfigurement of small- and medium-sized trees. Trees with sturdy trucks are seldom chosen by bucks for rubbing.

IT'S ALL ABOUT FUNGI!!!

Creating a fungal-rich environment for your pawpaw trees above and below ground will help them thrive. Most of our fruit trees evolved in woodland settings rich in organic matter and fungi. Fungi break down organic matter into bioavailable nutrients for plants. This can be achieved by simply adding deep layers of organic material (woodchips, straw, mulch) in a 5- to 10-foot diameter around each tree. The fungal-rich environment that is created by deeply layering organic matter supports the soil food web, while helping maintain the high moisture levels where pawpaw trees thrive. Plus, this environment also cushions the falling fruit. Be generous with your mulching, as it will quickly break down. Try to consistently maintain four or more inches of mulch, as this will dramatically reduce your long-term inputs and maximize tree health and productivity. Adding a mycorrhizal inoculant to the root zone also assures strong fungal networks that boost tree health and resilience. See more about fungi in Appendix I: Pawpaw and Permaculture.

Important note: Adding woodchips or other organic mulches to the surface around plantings does not lock up nutrients to the root zone; rather, this happens when undigested organic matter is mixed in with soil. Tests have shown that black walnut and cedar wood chips will not adversely affect trees when used as a mulch. So . . . mulch away!

Wyatt "Fungi" Judd holding an edible
giant Wine Cap mushroom!

ECO-LOGICAL TREE FEEDING

② ADD COMPANION PLANTS

NITROGEN FIXER

POLLINATOR

MULCH

INSECTARY

① START WITH DEEP MULCHING

STRAW

WOODCHIPS

CARDBOARD

NEWSPAPER

COMPOST

GROUNDCOVER

WOOD ASH

ROCK DUST

CHARCOAL

③ ADD MANURE AND AMENDMENTS ANNUALLY

CHAPTER 5

ECO-LOGICAL TREE CARE

The value of early shaping cannot be overemphasized. It makes a huge difference in managing the tree for the duration of its life, balancing the tree's leaf ratio with a full, yet uncrowded, canopy.

One of the pawpaw's greatest attributes is that it can be a carefree, low-input fruit tree. Once established in a suitable site, this is often the case; however, to ensure steady fruit harvest and ease of access, some tree care is needed.

We have trees here on our homestead that were roughly heeled in 20 years ago in poor, but draining, soil; these trees have thrived with no care. They look beautiful and have lived a fine existence without any human input beyond planting. The catch, though, is that they are 20-feet tall and do not bear fruit consistently every year. Most of the fruit they do bear are not accessible without a very tall ladder!

If easily harvesting this fruit and maximizing fruit quality are your goals, then this section is for you. If you're just wanting to try a carefree fruit tree option without attachment to harvest outcomes, you can follow the basics for establishment and forget about it.

Feeding

Under heavy production, pawpaw trees need consistent nutrients to maintain quality fruit and overall tree health. When pawpaws are pumping out 30 or more pounds of plump fruit per tree, they are pulling resources from the soil that need replenishing.

Chemical inputs are easy upfront but complicated downstream, so I am going to focus on ecological[1] and organic feeding methods.

With productive pawpaw trees, your inputs will be relative to the outputs. This can be minimal on both ends or designed to balance your time and energy from moderate to high input. Minimal would involve mulching and drawing in fungi, previously covered in Chapter 4. So, let's start with moderate.

Moderate inputs rely largely on companion planting. Getting your companion plants and ground covers established early around pawpaw trees can reduce your maintenance dramatically and provide ongoing services, such as moisture retention, weed block, soil building, nutrient cycling, and a beneficial habitat for insect ecology. Setting it up right, along with the natural cycles, will maintain and improve bio-functions. Really, it does work!

Companion Planting

In permaculture, we work with "guilds," which are sets of companion plants that form a supportive ecology for fruit and nut trees. Guild-building is flexible and largely dependent on your plant interests and uses, as long as certain benefits or "services" are being passed along. For example, having nitrogen-fixing plants in the guild is important for ongoing feeding needs; mulching plants and ground covers help hold moisture, reduce weeds, and add nutrient-rich organic material; while flowering plants draw in pollinators and beneficial insects.

Ideally, you would add companion plants into an existing compost or mulch the whole area around the tree once all your plantings are in place. With good companion plant establishment, the ongoing need for mulch will be taken care of by the plants themselves; however, mulching at the beginning is helpful in getting all plantings to thrive.

At a minimum with my pawpaw tree plantings, I include a nitrogen-fixing plant and a "mulch" plant to help establish the tree's needs up front and build diversity. Nitrogen-fixing plants pull nitrogen gas out of the air and fix it in the root zone, where it hangs out in little

---

1 An ecological approach mimics nature's patterns of interwoven systems based on organic matter, fungi, and plant symbiosis. The ecological approach takes minor forethought and design, and then largely maintains itself.

fertilizer-containing pellets (a.k.a., root nodules) that are bio-available for neighboring roots to take up. This bio-available form of nitrogen right in the root zone is perfect for easy absorption. I plant my nitrogen-fixing plants close to the root zone of the young trees, within one to two feet, to meet fertility needs up front. I call these nitrogen-fixers "nurse" plants, as they feed and mulch the tree as it grows—thus, nursing it—and eventually phasing out with the tree's successful establishment. Nitrogen-fixers are often plants in the pea family (legumes) that have a wide range of useful and ornamental choices to match your needs and aesthetics.

On the low-key side of soft perennials—those that die back to the ground each year—are blue false indigo (*Baptisia australis*) and lupins (*Lupinus*); they are attractive and low maintenance. For more vigorous nitrogen-fixers, I like woody perennials such as lead plant (*Amorpha canescens*), bundle flower (*Desmanthus illinoensis*), and black locust (*Robinia pseudoacacia*), the latter of which can also double as an early shade tree for sapling pawpaw trees. With larger woody nitrogen-fixing plants, you will need to cut them back once your pawpaw trees do not need shading. Be ready and willing to manage this key role or your "nurse" will hog the space. When a nitrogen-fixer is cut back during the growing season, its benefits are twofold, as it both drops mulch and releases nitrogen nodules into the root zone. Setting up nitrogen-fixing plants with young trees is a key move to strong establishment and low maintenance.

Mulch plants also aid in successful tree establishment and low maintenance by shading and feeding the topsoil with their nutrient-rich leaves and stems, while keeping back weeds and diversifying insect habitat. That is a lot of services!

Year 3 (left): Two pawpaws sittin'on a swale . . . with a nitrogen-fixing lead plan snuggled in between.
Year 6 (right): Lead plant phased out as pawpaw trees mature.

"Chop and drop" is a popular saying and practice in permaculture that refers to cutting back the top vegetative growth of vigorously growing plants and allowing the material to fall as mulch. It is simply mulch that is planted in place. Once established, mulch plants can replace the need to bring in straw and wood chips, as these plants create a living mulch to provide the services of weed control, moisture retention, and organic matter for the soil. Some plants, such as comfrey and horseradish, will drop their overgrowth naturally on their own; chopping them two or three times a season can quicken the soil-building process and help stimulate multiple flowerings to benefit pollinators. Nettles are another good mulch plant; be sure to sow them in their own area, unless you like getting zapped while picking pawpaws![*]

*Cut comfrey and nettle make a great liquid fertilizer high in nutrients and minerals. Simply fill a five-gallon bucket with cut plant material and water, let sit for three days, and use as a soil drench.

My favorite mulch plant, by far, is comfrey.[2] Comfrey is a beautiful, soft perennial with luxurious, large, and abundant deep green leaves. It has copious flowers and a willingness to grow in both full shade and full sun. Comfrey is a very easy-to-grow plant that asks very little, yet gives so much. Comfrey is known as a "dynamic accumulator," meaning its deep tap root pulls up minerals and nutrients from the subsoil into its leaves; when the plant is cut back or dies down, it mulches and releases these nutrients all around your trees. Comfrey shoots out of the ground very early in spring and is one of the first plants to flower and offer nectar to solitary bees. It is a phenomenal medicinal plant, to boot!

Some of my other favorite mulch plants that have multiple benefits are rhubarb, horseradish, yarrow, and lemon balm. Ultimately, choose mulch plants that you will harvest and utilize, offering the greatest ecological services for those "helpers" you love most: bees, earthworms, spiders, etc.

Ground Covers: The Ultimate Living Mulch

Ground covers are great service providers, as they prevent erosion, weeds, and moisture loss while promoting diversity. These spreaders can do a lot of work for you by colonizing open ground that otherwise would need to be managed for weeds. The process of ground cover plants growing and dying back each season "pulses" soil growth by adding organic matter above and below the surface, while creating food

2   I work with three different types of comfrey: *Symphytum x uplandicum,* the common stand-alone Russian Comfrey that reaches 3-feet tall; *Symphytum Hidcote Blue,* which is a spreading comfrey that grows 18- to 24-inches tall; and *Symphytum tuberosuma,* a rare low-growing comfrey that grows white flowers and spreads, yet only reaches a height of 12 inches. Love, love, love these guys!

Running comfrey "Hidcote Blue" makes a great ground cover for pawpaw patches

and shelter for soil biota. You can speed up the natural pulsing process by chopping and dropping the plants just after flowering. Many ground covers, such as mints and comfrey, also double as important pollinators for bees and other beneficial insects.

I have roughly three acres of established food forests with around 60 pawpaw trees that require very little of my time. This is in large part due to my extensive use of ground covers. Where I have successfully established ground covers—and where I have not—becomes quickly evident by the amount of labor I have to put in. In areas with significant ground cover, I have very low weed-management needs. The downside of many ground covers is that you lose some diversity by having only one or two plant varieties versus filling the space with multiple companion plants. I find ground covers are best suited to larger landscape designs, or for those who have little time and interest to manage an array of plants.

Ground covers establish well when following the planned planting regime outlined in Chapter 4. The broken-down mulch provides a good medium to establish some of my favorite ground covers, such as Creeping St. John's Wort (*Hypericum calycinum*), fuki (*Petastes japonicus*), spreading comfreys, mints, white clover, and strawberries.

WHAT THE FUK! *IS* THAT?

A favorite ground cover plant at our Long Creek Homestead in Frederick, Maryland, is fuki (*Petasites japonicus*), a traditional Japanese perennial vegetable whose young spring stalks are cherished in the native culture. Lucky for us, the local deer population do not care for it! Fuki's large leaves and quick establishment create a shaded soil around our pawpaw trees that helps to maintain consistent moisture levels and abundant organic matter for long-term soil building, plus it's fun to chop and drop!

If you plant your fuki along with your sapling pawpaw trees, be sure to keep up with the chop and drop around the young trees. I have seen fuki cover over trees smaller than two or three feet. Once the trees are three feet or more, the fuki can fill in around the tree and keep lower branches from forming, a positive since low branches heavy with fruit can lay on the ground and get funky quickly. Fuki will do well to stay within areas that are mowed around, but it will spread if left unchecked.

Water and Fertility

For full and consistent harvests, trees need heavy nutrient inputs and consistent water availability.

Don't let that sentence scare you! It is not as dramatic as it sounds. Keeping up with trees that produce high-quality fruit does require attention and timely inputs. The key is to assure that your soil health and trees can keep up with fruit production. Pawpaw trees are heavy feeders of nitrogen, potassium, iron, zinc, magnesium, sulfur, and calcium. The following is my way to approach fertility needs.[3]

Water—The Most Essential Ingredient!

Let's start with water, as it is the most essential ingredient for all nutrient uptake. Pawpaw trees use a lot of water, especially when plumping up and maturing fruits. Many climates in the pawpaw's natural range have adequate moisture for good fruit production, and there are ways to ensure this moisture in case of drought or for areas that are drier than the ideal. Thick mulch acts like a sponge for rain falling on it and for any runoff it catches. I find 6 to 8 inches of wood chips in an 8- to 10-foot diameter around each tree holds sufficient moisture in climates receiving 30 or more inches of rain per year.[4] If pawpaw trees are grouped together, the entire area can be heavily mulched to magnify moisture retention. Setting up an island like this offers a good opportunity for adding in companion plantings and other small fruits such as black currant bushes. The ultimate water harvesting comes from creating earthworks that passively harvest rainwater into the ground uphill from your plantings. (See Swales on Contour in Appendix I: Pawpaws and Permaculture for details.) Drip irrigation is my last choice, as it is often a large investment and uses plastic

---

3 Because feeding regimes vary widely, I am adding the disclaimer that other farmers may have different and equally successful ways to fertilize and manage their pawpaw trees.

4 Bona fide studies have shown that thick mulches as high as 10 inches do not negatively affect trees (unless piled up against the trunk), nor do they tie up nitrogen in the soil.

Deep mulch and companion plants go a far way to support tree growth by holding moisture and cycling nutrients. Pictured here is a one-year-old pawpaw sapling protected by an 18-inch tree tube and wire fence, deeply mulched, along with a companion planting of running comfrey— which, after just one season, will cover the patch.

non-biodegradable resources. And, if not carefully calibrated in clay soils, there is risk of overwatering and rotting the roots. That said, many growers use drip irrigation successfully with pawpaws.

Fertilizer—The Second Most-Essential Ingredient

I fertilize my pawpaw trees anytime from leaf fall in the autumn until June, but avoid fertilizing July through early autumn. Fertilizing too late in the growing season—July, August, or September—can stimulate excessive growth that cannot harden off properly before winter. Many growers, especially those using fast-release fertilizers, will fertilize during early autumn, once leaves have dropped, and then again in spring when roots are actively growing. For feeding established trees, I apply a generous five- to six-inch layer of aged, but not leached, manure on top of my wood chips around the entire root zone. For my pawpaw trees surrounded by ground covers, I reduce my manure application to a max of four inches to avoid smothering them, and only apply while they are dormant. (Note that nutrient-rich compost can be used in lieu of manure; however, many pawpaw growers choose to use both.)

Following the manure and/or compost application, I then generously spread wood ash[5] to help add potassium (which pawpaws use heavily), rock dust as a remineralizer, and bits of burned charcoal. The charcoal acts as small receptacles for nutrients and beneficial soil critters. You can make your own charcoal, which is popularly called bio-char, or go around collecting from fireplaces and fire pits. Ideally, inoculate the charcoal so it can soak up nutrients before being added as a fertilizer by letting it sit in your compost or manure pile for a few months before adding it as a fertilizer. Charcoal can go a long way toward preventing your nutrients from leaching out quickly. Thick mulch under the manure also helps absorb and hold nutrients longer, and then covering your manure or compost protects the nutrients from volatizing.

There are many manure options to work with. I have many trees, so I work with what is most locally abundant from healthy situations: mainly local small-scale horse farms that do not use excessive antibiotics and dewormers. Horses are often kept in stalls with wood shavings or straw as bedding, upon which they pee and poop. This ready-made compost mix of carbon and nitrogen is mucked out into large piles often ready for the taking. I try to get my manure soon after it's been mucked out, re-pile it in the shade near my trees, then cover the pile with a piece of old burlap, and allow it to decompose further before applying. The burlap helps slow down leaching from heavy rains, plus hold a consistent moisture for the manure. Unfortunately, I often see large piles of uncovered manure piled in the open air with a steady stream of coffee-colored water seeping out the bottom; this is the natural fertilizer running away into the watershed.

I let my fresh manure compost for six to eight weeks before applying it around my trees. If the manure pile you source from has been sitting for a couple of months, then it is ready to apply right away. The trick is to not apply manure while it is still strong in nitrogen as it can burn the roots, though this is less likely when applying over a generous bed of mulch. Cow manure is considered a "cold" manure and can be applied directly around trees when nice and fresh. Heads up: Horse manure often contains weed seeds if not properly composted.

For those without access to bulk manures or just not wanting to deal with the heavy workload that gathering, composting, and spreading entails, then chicken manure is where it's at. Chicken manure has a higher NPK[6] content than most animal manures, so aside from the nitrogen, you get good shots of phosphorus and potassium as well. Be aware, though, that chicken manure is very "hot" when fresh, having a very high nitrogen level that may damage plants. Fortunately, there is a strong market for dried chicken manure, so it is available in manageable bags ready for easy application. Spreading chicken manure as a fertilizer is very effective and relatively light work. The downside with chicken manure is that you don't get all the fibers and organic matter that comes with the larger animal manures, which helps build a healthy soil tilth.

---

5 If you have a balanced pH of 7 or higher, adding wood ash is not recommended as it can raise pH levels. For pawpaws, the typical high limit of pH is 7, though there are reports of healthy pawpaw trees growing at a pH of 7.5.
6 NPK is the relative content of the macronutrients nitrogen (N), phosphorus (P), and potassium (K).

Soil testing before planting, during growth, and through productive years will give helpful guidance to what additional nutrients may be needed. Once trees are established and growing well, your chosen soil lab[7] can test the leaves using a leaf assay in order to give you feedback on what the trees need. Most soil labs will not have a baseline for pawpaw, but they are similar for apple if they need a reference crop to run the test, except that pawpaws like slightly more acid soil. For serious growers, soil and leaf samples should be taken every couple of years to avoid elemental deficiencies. That said, I take most lab-generated soil and leaf results as a rough outline to see if there are any strong markers out of place and to translate their conventional adjustment recommendations into organic supplements. For example, if my leaf assay shows that the trees are low in potassium and recommends a strong fertilizer concentrate, I will apply a liquid seaweed fertilizer spray to the trees for a quick boost, then add in greensand or granite dust to help for ongoing slow release of potassium, then ultimately plant more comfrey to cycle the potassium needs naturally. If adding additional fertility supplements, I typically do so when laying down manure.

Unless you have some awesomely rich soil, be sure to design a fertility plan; otherwise, you risk the tree weakening and declining. This is especially true with the large fruited varieties, as they can pull many nutrients from the soil in order to make those big, lush luscious fruits. Signs of deficiencies and tree decline include: low vigor; branch dieback; leaves showing signs of chlorosis[8] or yellowing around the fruit; high susceptibility to disease and insects; and, of course, sudden death.

MULCH SANDWICH

Each year, I add more wood chips and manure under my trees so that I get a layered effect—a "mulch sandwich," if you will—that creates a balance of nitrogen and carbon to support soil biota and fungi. Ultimately, this mulch sandwich makes nutrients available for your trees.

Rates of feeding will vary based on tree age and specific site where the tree is planted. I only use compost, mulch, and a homemade "green tea" for the first year of tree establishment to help keep the focus on root development versus fast top growth. Green tea is a simple plant-based liquid fertilizer I make by packing a five-gallon bucket two-thirds full with leaves of comfrey and stinging nettle, then filling with water, and allowing to sit three or four days. I then use the nutrient-rich tea to drench the soil around my young trees, about a half bucket per tree. If you mash the plants before adding water, this will release more nutrients, as does stirring the plants each day. Between comfrey and nettles, you get a good mix of macro nutrients and minerals in a soluble form that tree roots can easily absorb. If you don't have comfrey or nettles, use whatever nutrient-rich plants you have growing. After the first year of establishment,

---

7 Most states have a soil testing lab that you go through your county agricultural extension agent to use.

8 Chlorosis is a condition in which leaves produce insufficient chlorophyll, which is responsible for the green color of leaves. Note: leaf chlorosis near the fruit can be a result of mineral translocation within the tree from leaves to fruit, which is an aspect of tree wisdom and may not be a nutritional deficiency, provided the overall tree and leaf health looks good.

FRUIT THINNING

As hard as thinning your pawpaw fruits may be, it is a win-win for better fruit quality and tree health.[*]

Fruit thinning refers to removing excess fruits early in the growing season. Reasons for thinning fruit include:

- Allowing remaining fruits to fill out fully and receive more nutrients
- Increasing the tree's ability to form flower buds for the following year's harvest, which helps prevent biennial bearing (high production one year followed by a year of low yields)
- Reducing stress on the tree
- Disease control (especially fungal issues)
- Limiting limb breakage due to heavy harvest weight

Many fruit trees will naturally drop flowers and immature fruits to balance loads year to year based on prevailing weather and soil conditions but often need help, especially with heavy-producing cultivars.

Fruit thinning pawpaws is best done in early summer while fruit clusters are still itty bitty, with an additional light thinning in August. The goal is to have no more than three or four fruits per cluster. Start by removing any fruits on the ends of branches to lessen downward pull. This also helps reduce the potential for sunscald on fruit, which can cause skin damage and uneven ripening where one side of the fruit ripens early while the inside does not.

Pawpaws can cluster in groups of up to 9 fruits!

[*]Most home growers do not grasp the importance of fruit thinning and pruning for long-term tree health. Not only does thinning ultimately increase the amount of fruit, this process also helps your trees maintain a healthy balance and longevity.

adding nitrogen to the tea is helpful. Stay with me here . . . on the day you are ready to apply the tea, add your urine to the mix. Don't freak!! Along with trace amounts of vitamins and minerals, urine is high in urea, which is nitrogen. Add urine up to $\frac{1}{10}$ of the tea's volume, stir the mixture, and apply. See Appendix I: Pawpaws and Permaculture for details on water harvesting techniques.

Pruning and Shaping

You do not need to prune pawpaw trees if you are okay with a full-sized tree and fluctuating harvests, and can accept dangling fruit that hang just outside your reach.

We have a pair of beautiful, fully shaped 20-foot-tall pawpaw trees at our homestead that have never been pruned and, for most years, they have born much fruit. But half of that fruit is out of reach, and when it does come down, it's a smushy affair. I used to climb these trees for the tempting high-hanging fruit until one day I found myself dangling by one arm after the brittle branch I was perched on snapped![9] Stretching off a 10-foot step ladder can be equally dodgy. So, now I prune my pawpaw trees to around eight-feet high, where fruit can be easily picked with both my feet firmly on the ground. The moral of this little story is to keep your loved ones and yourself from undue stress by keeping your feet on the ground and the pawpaw fruit within reach!

One of my daily adventures includes combing the ground under the two 20-foot-tall beauties each morning during harvest season to collect fallen fruits that have not split open. I then freeze this harvest for future pulping (see Chapter 6 for the freezing process). If I get behind on picking up the fruit, they will rot quickly and draw unwanted flies and bees.

Fortunately, pruning pawpaw trees is not very challenging.

THE BENEFITS OF PRUNING

- Improve fruit quality
- Height reduction
- Disease reduction
- Ease of harvest
- Allow close spacing
- Select strong branching
- Avoid limb and fruit rubbing

---

9 A strong word of caution: Climbing pawpaw trees is not advised, as the branch wood is weak and can easily break under climbing or standing weight.

Thinning versus Heading

There are two types of pruning cuts—thinning and heading—which produce different effects. Thinning cuts remove the entire shoot or branch back to where it meets the branch or trunk. Heading cuts shorten a branch or shoot by pruning just a portion off the end. Heading cuts stimulate the remaining lateral buds on the branch to increase vigor and encourage the sprouting of new shoots that results in an explosion of dense growth that limits light and air flow within the tree. Typically, with fruit trees, you want to focus on thinning cuts to avoid crowding.

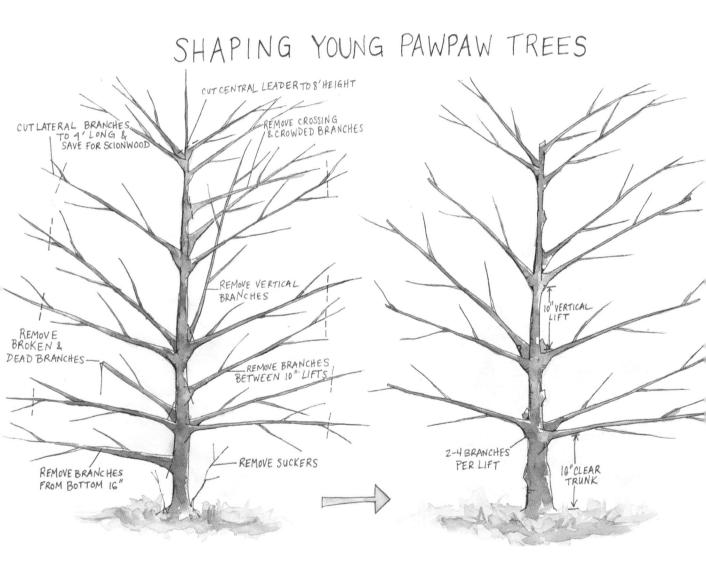

SHAPING YOUNG PAWPAW TREES

CUT CENTRAL LEADER TO 8' HEIGHT

REMOVE CROSSING & CROWDED BRANCHES

CUT LATERAL BRANCHES TO 4' LONG & SAVE FOR SCIONWOOD

REMOVE VERTICAL BRANCHES

REMOVE BROKEN & DEAD BRANCHES

REMOVE BRANCHES BETWEEN 10" LIFTS

REMOVE SUCKERS

REMOVE BRANCHES FROM BOTTOM 16"

10" VERTICAL LIFT

2-4 BRANCHES PER LIFT

16" CLEAR TRUNK

Building a Framework

The best time to prune pawpaw trees is in late winter or early spring when they are dormant. I wait until my trees are strongly established, usually between years four and six.[10] Usually by this time, the trees have reached a height of at least six feet. When trees are young, pruning is called "shaping," as your cuts will begin to direct the permanent framework. The first goal is thinning out crowded branches and removing branches that have vertical, narrow crotches. Limb spacing early on helps the tree build a strong framework that makes pruning in consecutive years much easier. Pawpaws have a natural growth pattern that is termed "central leader," meaning they have strong vertical growth versus a vase-like spread.

The first branches to remove are any that are crossing, broken, dead, leggy, or deformed. Next, prune any lateral branches with narrow crotch angles (that is, vertically inclined). The ideal crotch angle is between 45 and 60 degrees from the trunk; this broader angle helps promote a strong branch connection that will be less prone to break under the weight of fruit, snow, or wind. When trees are young and pliable, crotch angles can be encouraged by using limb spreaders; otherwise, cut them out. Removing low branches to 16 inches[11] off the ground at this stage is also recommended, as branches laden with fruit will droop to the ground allowing the fruit to get funky fast. This also opens air flow under the tree, gives access under the branches, and provides space for companion and groundcover plants to do their job.

Once the obvious pruning is managed, step back and look at the tree. Does it have strong, well-spaced branches? This can be hard to discern if there are many crowded branches. The goal at this stage is to select strong branches that are equally separated around the trunk and vertically spaced approximately 10 inches, which allows room for branches, side shoots, and leaves. Once you can visualize the framework you want, the branches needing to be pruned become clear.

Typically, you will select two to four branches around the tree at each vertical lift (interval) that point in different directions. Sometimes, the vertical lifts between the tree branchings are not so obvious; this is where applying your understanding of general spacing is essential so that branches do not collide as they grow and send out side shoots. The branches that are not part of the framework need to come out. Do not cut them flush with the trunk, because this will damage the branch "collar," which serves as a barrier to the decay of fungi and bacteria. Until the tree reaches eight-feet tall (in five to eight years), continue pruning out new branch shoots that are not part of the framework, along with any root suckers. If any of the upper lateral branches begin to compete with the central leader, prune them back to a side shoot to avoid having multiple leaders.

---

10 An exception to pruning in the first year or two is if the trees have been dug bare root or have been grown in small containers, then reducing top growth is useful to bring balance. This can be done by trimming back the lateral branches by one-third or removing a few branches completely.

11 As the tree matures, you will find the need to prune the lower branches higher to keep them lifted off the ground. A mature tree can easily have a 24- to 36-inch clear trunk to the lowest branch.

I cannot overemphasize the value of early shaping. It makes a huge difference in managing the tree for the duration of its life, balancing the tree's leaf ratio with a full, yet uncrowded, canopy.

Managing Height and Width

The next main goal in pruning pawpaws is to manage height and lateral branch length. I like to keep my pawpaw trees at an eight-foot height for easy harvest and management. Oftentimes trees will hit this height by the time I do my first shaping when they are four to six years old. I go more by the tree's growth than by age, as different sites and rootstock affect growth vigor and the need to shape.

Start by heading back the central leader to the uppermost lateral branch. This will direct the energy flow to all the lateral branches. Lateral branches should then be reduced in length to approximately four feet from the trunk. Make these reduction cuts ¼ inch past a side branch pointing in the direction you want growth to move since that branch will now get a shot of growth hormone from removing the branch end. Keeping your lateral branches to four feet helps branches deal with heavy fruit loads, maintains air flow, and allows for closer spacing (8 to 10 feet). Ideally, you do not want your trees to be touching each other or overlapping at all. Note, if you do not plan to prune your trees and have the space, be sure to place them 12- to 15-feet apart to avoid overlapping, or plant two together in the same hole and grow them out as "one tree."

Making these reduction cuts will result in extra regrowth that will need to be managed. The easiest time to address excessive new growth from reducing cuts is when they are still soft and can be easily pinched off during the growing season. Otherwise, in the next dormant pruning season, thin them out for air flow and ease of access. You will get new central leader growth; sometimes two or more central leaders will develop from cutting the top back. Continue to cut these central leaders back to approximately eight feet high. Note, if you begin this pruning process and stop doing it for a number of years, you will likely end up with multiple central leaders busting out the top, resulting in a tall, dense tree. It is easy to prune the trees if done so from the beginning. Root suckers can be pruned to the ground any time of year.

SCION GATHERING WHILE PRUNING

When pruning in late winter, you can collect the tips of the previous year's growth and save this as scion wood for grafting to other seedling pawpaw trees. The portion of the end branch that grew the previous year will be noted by the change in bark color and the presence of buds: it will be lighter in color and smoother looking. These prunings (i.e., scion wood) can be cut into 8-inch pieces and stored in a resealable plastic storage bag, along with a damp paper towel or newspaper, and placed in the refrigerator until the seedling trees begin to leaf out, at which time they can be grafted. Chapter 3 gives full details.

MIKE'S ALL-PURPOSE TREE-HEALING PAINT

If you want to take your tree paint to the next level, make this multipurpose salve to lather on your trees:

- Diluted milk paint or lime wash
- Finely sifted compost to add micro-nutrients, which speed tissue healing
- Diatomaceous earth, which has sharp edges to cut up crawling bugs
- Kaolin clay to smother overwintering eggs

I am going out on a limb here: an all-purpose healing paint may also reduce or eliminate the damage that boring insects can inflict.

How Much to Prune?

I find most people do not prune enough. Lack of experience leads to concern of hurting the tree. With managed fruit trees, this is not good as soon you will have a hard-to-manage mess. To a much lesser degree, some people over prune. Once your fruit tree is mature, you can use the 25% mass removal theory: generally, up to 25% removal of the total tree mass will not damage the long-term health of the tree. So, as you learn to prune and are likely in the category of not pruning enough, keep going until you see approximately 25% of the tree's total mass lying on the ground. This is especially true if your tree has missed pruning years and needs serious reduction; in this case, make sure 25% of the total mass is on the ground, but not more. Heavy pruning will lead to an explosion of new growth and much more work for the pawpaw grower; the ideal is steady pruning each year from a young age.

If, after years of not pruning, a heavy pruning occurs, then you risk sun burning the inner branches and exposed fruits; think of lily-white winter skin getting fully blasted in the summer sun! If this happens, you need to cover the branches with a reflective paint. The simplest recipe is to apply a half-and-half mixture of white, milk-based paint[12] and water. A hydrated lime wash mix can also work. This technique is also applied to tree trunks to avoid sunscald, which happens in winter when the direct rays of the sun strike the southern/southwestern side of the tree. During the day, the bark is warmed, causing expansion; at night, a sudden drop to a low temperature causes damage to cells in the bark. Splits in bark—whether from sunscald, weed whackers, or deer rubbing—create wounds that insects, fungi, and bacteria can use to enter the tree. Breathable tree paint can also be used to cover up large pruning cuts or as a general salve for any damage to the tree.

---

12 A natural, breathable paint is recommended versus a commercial tree sealer, which can have a negative effect by trapping moisture in the tree and inviting decay.

While white plastic trunk wraps are often employed as protective measures, be sure to only use in them in winter months; when left on during the growing season, they provide the perfect habitat and protection for boring insects.

Clean Cutting

Pruning is basically surgery performed on a tree; it requires sharp tools and clean cuts that do not invite infection. If you are tearing bark when you prune, stop and sharpen your tool; otherwise, you will damage the tree's tissue and leave it vulnerable to viruses, bacteria, fungi, and insects. Leaving nubs of branches over a quarter inch is too long; these nubs will require the tree to exert energy to internally seal off the extra stub, which then dies off, leaving an access point for insects and disease. Likewise, cutting into the trunk or main branch of the tree when pruning causes a wound that is very difficult for the tree to heal. Aim to leave an eighth- to a quarter-inch maximum nub when pruning and be sure it is cut at an angle so water does not sit on the nub causing it to rot.

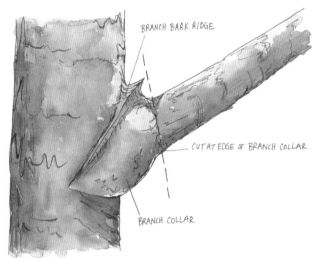

PROPER THINNING CUT

BRANCH BARK RIDGE

CUT AT EDGE OF BRANCH COLLAR

BRANCH COLLAR

Pruning correctly is not so difficult if you are being conscious and using sharp tools. To be sure you are doing no harm—or when pruning cuts go bad (this can happen to the best of us)—use a healing paint to cover the area.

I carry a pocket sharpener and bleach wipe in a sandwich bag with me when pruning to keep my tools sharp and clean. Alcohol also works well. It is recommended to clean your pruning tools with a disinfectant between trees so as not to transfer potential diseases.

Insect and Disease Issues

Pawpaws are one of the most disease- and insect-resistant fruit trees that you can grow.

The pawpaw produces potent bioactive compounds, known as annonaceous acetogenins, which naturally deter insects and critters alike. In fact, the pawpaw's acetogenins are being developed as effective natural insecticides and for fighting disease in cancer patients. Go Pawpaw!

That all sounds groovy, but the reality is that every species in the web of life eats and is eaten. The pawpaw is not exempt, it just has a very adaptive spirit . . . and acetogenins.

Disease and insect pressure are highest on fruit trees that are stressed and lack ecological diversity in the vicinity. This is largely why disease and insect issues vary site to site. My general approach to reducing disease and insect damage is to set up resilient conditions that naturally strengthen and balance the tree to hold its own under pressure.

I have found that growing pawpaw trees in a diverse habitat with good air flow, drainage, and healthy soil manages most major issues in regard to insect damage or plant disease. Weakened trees are more susceptible to disease and insect pressure.

A diverse habitat means having perennial cover for beneficial critters such as praying mantis, frogs, assassin bugs, and lizards, so that they can help sort out the would-be marauders. Perennial covers can be woody shrubs, piles of rocks (herb spirals), stacks of woody mate-

Caterpillar of the Zebra Swallowtail Butterfly

rial (hügelkultur beds), swale basins, deep woodchips, and ground cover plants. Having a tidy, tucked away landscape offers little to no habitat for beneficial species, and you will be left to deal with marauders solo! Many beneficial insects need to feed from small flowers with shallow, exposed nectaries, such as yarrow, black-eyed Susan, and mountain mint. Plant these, too.

The use of pesticides, herbicides, or fungicides is a lack of good design. If you are drawn to using chemicals, even strong "natural" ones, please take time to further your learning and understanding of ecosystem dynamics and permaculture practices. Using chemicals to address insect imbalances will only further compound the issue and negatively affect pollinators.

Critters

The following insects, animals, and disease issues are a collective of possible circumstances. The likeliness of them all combining is low, so please read with awareness rather than mounting concern.

The insect that gets the most attention, and rightly so, is the beautiful Zebra Swallowtail butterfly, for which the pawpaw tree is the soul host. Leaf damage from the larva of the Zebra Swallowtail is generally mild and well tolerated by us, due to the wondrous beauty of the striking black and white and red butterfly. That said, the stripy larvae can defoliate young seedlings. At our homestead, so far, the damage from the leaf chewing larvae in our pawpaw plant nursery has been minor. An interesting side note is that the Zebra Swallowtail gains an invincibility by eating the pawpaw leaves, as traces of acetogenins remain in their bodies, thus rendering them unpalatable to predators.

The Zebra Swallowtail Butterfly (*Eurytides marcellus*)

Pawpaw Peduncle Borer (*Talponia plummeriana*), a small native moth about a quarter-inch long, is a character of note and challenge. In spring, as the pawpaw blossoms open, the female moth lays her eggs upon the dense ball of stamens. The itty bitty larvae hatch and proceed to devour the center of the flower; after which, they burrow down the flower stem into the wood, and continue chewing their way downward. Once thought only to eat the pawpaw flower, this little voracious borer is occasionally showing up in the roots and fruit of the pawpaw. The main effect of the borer is the loss of flowers; in good years, this can be helpful to thin heavy fruit set, and in bad years, it can destroy the majority of flowers and fruit. At our homestead, we have evidence of the Peduncle Borer, but—thankfully—no significant damage to fruit or trees.

Do be aware of the potential to spread the Peduncle Borer to other trees. Since the Peduncle Borer lives out its pupal stage in the stems of year's growth, which is also the wood taken for scion, care must be taken not to ship grafting wood with these critters hitchhiking along.

The Pawpaw Webworm – This caterpillar feeds on pawpaw leaves, buds, and twigs during late summer and early autumn. They feed in groups, rolling up leaves with silk, and make a nasty-looking mess of branch ends. Fortunately, because their action is late in the season, little damage is done to the tree's health. Removing by hand and squishing underfoot is very effective for control.

Pawpaws are a delicacy enjoyed by many species!

The Ambrosia Beetle is a new character showing up on the pawpaw scene. Many species of Ambrosia Beetles exist, and all are "cosmopolitan," which means they feed on many different tree species instead of being confined to a single host—very often the case in the insect world. Pawpaw-growing guru Jim Davis says the presence of the Ambrosia Beetle is a good indicator that trees are being planted in a poorly drained soil. In wet soil, pawpaw roots will begin to rot and ferment, basically making alcohol, which can help draw in the Ambrosia Beetle. Though the beetles are more likely to attack weakened trees, they have been noted to enjoy a good munch on healthy trees, too. The beetles make their way into the tree's sapwood causing wilting of the foliage on the terminals of infested twigs and branches. Obvious signs of the Ambrosia Beetle are toothpick-like strands of sawdust sticking out from their tunnels and corresponding wet spots from sap leaking. Painting tree trunks may help deter these voracious critters.

Slugs, snails, Japanese beetles, and stink bugs can also take their toll if pressure is high, and especially in nursery situations with numerous young trees and soft new leaves. Again, having a diverse habitat for beneficial predators is the best approach to managing damage. Timely use of kaolin clay as a foliar spray can go far in keeping these characters moving along. Interestingly, while slugs are a true pest of pawpaw foliage in California and Europe, they almost never do damage in their native range.

Opposums, raccoons, skunks, and squirrels relish the pawpaw fruit! Here in our Appalachian holler, we have all of the above-mentioned critters and find that they mostly go for the ripened fallen fruit, of which there is plenty, and leave the hanging fruit for us to hand pick. Note: as fallen fruit can have scat and other wild animal funk on it, be sure to disinfect before consuming or sharing. Deer damage seems restricted to the bucks rubbing their antlers on exposed stretches of the trunk. Bears can break branches and pull down fruit, but like most animals, they are not into under ripe pawpaw fruit.

Diseases

There's fungus among us! Which is generally a good thing, but there are funky fungi. Fortunately, the pawpaw tree has co-evolved and become largely resilient to funky fungi.

Exceptions are numerous fungal strains that show up as brown/ black spots on leaves and black spots/blotches on fruit, generally only causing significant damage during periods of heavy rainfall and extended high humidity. The damage is superficial, not penetrating below the skin. Chief among them are *Phyllosticta asminae, Rhopalo-conidium asiminae,* and *Mycocentrospora asiminae.*

A fungal medley on the pawpaw fruit

Jim Davis, the long-time pawpaw orchardist, collectively calls the fungal medley that causes black spots on the fruit simply "tar spot." Horticulturists call it "sooty blotch" and "fly speck." When tar spot is extensive on fruit, it creates a hardened area that can lead to splitting[13] as the fruit matures. Jim has also noted at his orchard that the larger variety fruits split during heavy rainfall years; however, he has noted that the smaller fruited PA Golden variety resists splitting.

Fungal spots that do not lead to cracking are merely aesthetic issues and do not affect the pulp inside. Fungal disease issues are best managed by encouraging good air flow through pruning and adequate spacing, and by creating ideal soil conditions with proper drainage and ground cover. Thinning fruit in tight clusters can also help reduce fungal tar spots.

---

13 Fruit splitting can happen to peaches, apples, and other fruit.

CHAPTER 6

THE ART OF HARVEST: FRUIT HANDLING AND PROCESSING

....

Educating folks on how to work with the pawpaw fruit so that
it is a positive experience is important, as mishandling
pawpaws can quickly lead to poor results.

Harvesting

There are millions of wild pawpaws growing and fruiting in over 26 states in the U.S., and yet most people seem mystified that this fruit even exists! A number of factors explain this mystification, a large one being the dearth of understanding around harvesting. One reason I had for writing this manual is to help educate folks on how to work with the pawpaw fruit so that it is a positive experience, as mishandling pawpaws can quickly lead to poor results.

Your first experience with eating a pawpaw makes a lasting impression. This can be a love story or a total turn off. Which one it will be is greatly affected by quality and ripeness of the fruit. Hand-picking and eating a perfectly ripe pawpaw from a tree with good genetics can be an exquisite experience that combines custard-like pulp with floral aromas and sweet notes, transporting you on a tropical daydream. On the other hand, there may be a pawpaw fruit from a random tree that has fallen to the ground, been bruised, and sat in the sun for three days before someone comes along thinking, "Oh boy, I've finally found a pawpaw," only to experience a fruit with a discolored and mushy texture, funky aromas, and bitter notes. In short, timing and handling are key to a positive pawpaw experience.

The ideal is to hand-pick pawpaw fruit. Hand-picking pawpaws is part science and part art—one that involves a fair amount of fondling. Pawpaw fruit remains dead hard and green until it is almost ripe, and then it ripens very quickly. Depending upon the cultivar, pawpaw fruits may or may not change color to signal they are ripe; those that do will change color when ripening, moving from a solid green to light green to yellowish. This is commonly called color break. The key is to observe and feel the fruit daily as the ripening season begins by gently squeezing the fruit—as you would a peach—to test for softening. When the pawpaw is just beginning to ripen, the yield from finger pressure will be subtle, but enough so you can sense it is not rock hard anymore. If it has been ripening on the tree for a few days, it will be obviously soft to the light squeeze. This is where being gentle with your testing is key, as the fruit will bruise very easily once ripe. Any bruised areas of the fruit will ripen and rot quickly, usually within 24 hours. You don't want just anybody fondling your pawpaws!

Pawpaw Picking Season

Generally speaking, pawpaws have a harvest time spread out over a two- to four-week period, ranging from late summer through the first frost in autumn. Climate, weather, location, and genetics each play a role in pawpaw harvest time, which varies from region to region. In North America, this can range from July in the warmest reaches of the Deep South to October in the coolest reaches near the Great Lakes, with September generally being the prime harvest time in central pawpaw country.

Warmth and moisture are the two biggest climatic factors affecting pawpaw fruit harvest; in any given region, the harvest dates will fluctuate year to year. For example, at our homestead in central Maryland (prime pawpaw country), we generally have long, warm, and humid summers with approximately

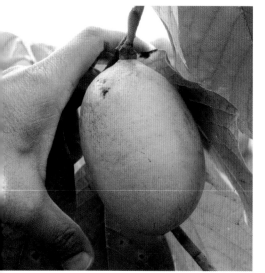

200 frost-free days. A typical year brings our harvest time mainly in the month of September, with the second and third week being peak; we do keep in mind that this can shift a week or two in either direction, depending on seasonal weather.

If you're not eating your freshly harvested pawpaw fruit right away, be sure to handle it carefully, as any impact will bruise the flesh. For prime grade fruit, do not pile pawpaws on top of each other; rather, place them in a single layer in your harvest bin or box, as even their own weight will cause damage—that is how easily a ripe pawpaw can bruise!

Spreading a thick layer of fresh straw under your pawpaw trees just before harvest season helps cushion fruit that falls in between hand-picking sessions. Note that fruit already fallen to the ground are usually quite ripe and will have a very short shelf life. Eat or process these fallen fruits right away.

Fruits can be picked when the earliest signs of ripening are detected and then left to ripen at room temperature (a quick process) or refrigerated (for slower maturation). At room temperature, a pawpaw that is just starting to ripen will mature to perfection in 24 to 36 hours. A fragrant, fruity aroma will be detected; the flesh will be firm and evenly textured; and the light, sweet notes of flavor will reward your senses in delightful ways. At 48 hours at room temperature, the fruit texture will be considerably soft and more custard-like; the flavor and aroma notes will be rich and deep. At 72 hours of ripening at room temperature, the fruit skin and flesh become discolored and very soft, and flavors tend toward rich, bitter notes of caramel and coffee—believe it or not, this is how some folks like their pawpaws! If your pawpaw makes it to day four inside, throw it in the compost and hope that next year new seedlings will sprout. Knowing how you like your pawpaw fruit to taste will drive the time you allow it to ripen.

Pawpaw fruit can be born singly or in clusters of up to nine per bunch. Some cultivars turn a lighter green/yellow when ripe, while others do not change color at all.

You may ask, "But, Michael, what if I don't want to eat my pawpaw right away?" No worries! There are two solutions: (1) refrigerating your harvest and (2) pulping and freezing your fruit.

If you intend to enjoy eating your fruit in the next week or so after harvesting, put it in the refrigerator right away. It may be held this way for one to three weeks, depending on maturation going in.

If fruit is picked before the ripening process has begun, it will stay hard and not ripen. If you try eating an under-ripe pawpaw, you will likely end up with a serious tummy ache! There is a story that gets repeated around pawpaw harvest season where some eager soul heads out to pick pawpaws without knowing about the fruit's ripeness window. Often this well-intended soul plucks under-ripe fruit from wild trees, returns home and excitedly shares this uncommon fruit with friends and family. A few hours later, there is a line to the bathroom! Worse is when this soul takes their under-ripe pawpaws to a local café owner who, likewise, does not know how to work with the pawpaw, yet is excited to hop on the pawpaw band wagon. The café owner prepares a pawpaw dish and hypes it up. Low and behold, it is a disaster. When the word gets out that folks got sick eating pawpaws, both the café owner and the fruit get a bum rap. Likewise, scooping half-rotted pawpaws off the ground and sharing with newbies also distorts the fruit's reputation.

Some over-enthusiastic harvesters resort to tree shaking; while this technique works, it will bruise the fruit as it hits the ground. If you are eating or processing the fruit right away, then the tree-shaking method is a sure time saver. Ripening pawpaws easily come off their stems, so trees need only be gently

Prime harvests of 35 pounds (and sometimes more) per tree occur when ideal moisture, good soil conditions, and warm temperatures combine. It's good to keep some good whiskey on hand to celebrate the harvest!

shaken, otherwise you risk causing unripe pawpaws to drop to the ground. Bruised fruit will ripen unevenly and spoil quickly, so be ready to use them immediately.

Safe Handling

Certain wild animals are pawpaw fruit aficionados. Sometimes, they have all-out parties in the pawpaw patch during harvest season. A wild party is a messy affair that leaves behind certain deposits . . . some of which are hazardous to human health. While I will spare you the details, I will clearly emphasize that fruit picked off the ground could have undesirable funk on it that should be properly washed and disinfected before being consumed. While there are numerous fruit and vegetable washes on the market today, a homemade vinegar wash—three parts vinegar to one part water—usually does the job. Just be sure to wipe the fruit clean so you don't get vinegar-flavored pawpaws!

Note that soil infertility can affect harvest by lowering fruit set and causing premature fruit drop. Some average harvest times noted in the U.S. include:

- Louisiana: late July to early September
- North Carolina: early August to mid-September
- Missouri: early September to early October
- Ohio: early September to early October
- New York[1]: late September to mid-October
- Washington State: October

FACTORS AFFECTING SEASONAL HARVEST

- Cool and cloudy summers, which can delay fruit ripening.
- Wet weather, which increases fruit splitting and bring on fungal issues.
- Drought, making fruit ripen early and fall from the tree more quickly.
- Wind and storms that can knock fruits en masse to the ground.

---

1 For those in the colder states (zones 4/5), such as upstate New York, fruit may get hit with frost and never ripen. And those regions with warm summer days but cool nights can also end up with unripe fruit at seasons end.

Foraging

You don't have to be a hairy, hippy, mushroom-jerky-eating forager to easily score wild pawpaws. Within the naturalized range, pawpaws grow abundantly. They may well be found along bike paths, urban parks, suburban woodland patches, or—as I recently discovered—ringing a cemetery. Pawpaws often hide in plain sight. Look near waterways, an obvious start, but you will likely find just as many growing in upland areas where there is sufficient moisture and wind protection.

Fruit explorer Ryan Lambert finds a score of ripe pawpaws along the C&O Canal near the town of Pawpaw, West Virginia

The easiest time of year to spot pawpaw trees is in autumn when their big green leaves turn golden yellow. Though this usually occurs after harvest time, it is helpful for identifying trees for the following year. The fruits are a giveaway too, although they can be hard to see under the dense foliage, especially when unripe and green. Most likely, the wild harvested fruits will be small—two or three inches long by about an inch wide—typically not like the big honking beauties you get on select cultivator trees. That is not to say there are not some large, gorgeous, very tasty fruit to be foraged; indeed, most of the named cultivars are from savvy foragers with keen observation, but even many of the little fruits are excellently flavored. Just beware that there are some bitter, musky, wild pawpaws lurking out there. Don't be that person who perpetuates funky fruit—leave it to the raccoons!

If you do plan to share or sell foraged pawpaw fruit, please know what you are doing. Under-ripe pawpaws equal a belly ache and ground-harvested fruit can be contaminated.

Storing and Processing

Ripening pawpaws pump out large quantities of ethylene gas, a plant hormone that stimulates ripening metabolism, which means ripe pawpaws do not store fresh for very long. Under ideal conditions, when pawpaws are hand-picked just prior to being fully ripened, and not bruised in transit, they can be kept in refrigeration (34°F) for up to three weeks, but typically a ripe pawpaw fruit will only last one week in refrigeration. While pawpaws are not like apples that can be stored for a long time, the good news is that pulped pawpaw fruit freezes well.

Pulping pawpaws is a learned art. My family used to pulp our fruit soon after picking; we split them in half, scooped out the pulp and seeds with a spoon, then mushed through the pulp to remove the remaining seeds. It took 15 minutes to pulp one fruit, and was it ever messy! Then we discovered the secret of freezing.

First, freeze the fruit whole (skin and all). Granted, you will need enough freezer space to hold the whole fruit. (Note: if you have too many fruit to put in the freezer at one time, you can hold some in the refrigerator up to a few days following harvest until you've processed the first batch.)

Once frozen solid (this takes no more than 12 hours), remove them from the freezer, then wait 20 to 30 minutes.

Peel the skin with a peeler, like you would a potato, then pry the slightly thawed flesh open. The seeds[2] pop out as clean as can be! If you don't wait the 20 to 30 minutes, the fruit won't pry open.

Once deseeded, pile your chunks of still mostly frozen pulp into resealable plastic freezer bags and pop them back in the freezer, where they can stay for up to two years.[3] Be sure to write the date of freezing on the bag to alleviate the guesswork.

When I get behind in pulping, I just leave the whole fruits in the freezer and come back sometimes months later to pulp. This eliminates a lot of pressure during harvest season when you quickly become inundated with fruit.

Whether you are pulping fresh or frozen, be sure to remove all the skin, as it adds bitter notes to the pulp. Some folks add a little lemon juice to the pulp to preserve its vibrant yellow color; however, if fruit is pulped and frozen quickly, the color should stay intact. If pulp is allowed to sit at room temperature for very long it will begin to oxidize and turn brown, much like a banana.

A step up from hand-processing is using a conical food mill or colander, where you have to really press

---

2 Note that this freezing method will drastically reduce the pawpaw seed viability for germination.

3 Unless you are planning a big event that will use a lot of pulp at once, consider freezing in one- or two-cup quantities. When frozen pulp thaws, it will oxidize quickly, so it's best to use as soon as possible or keep tightly sealed in the plastic bag until ready to enjoy.

the fruit to squeeze through the holes. Not a favorite approach at our place, but you may find it worth experimenting with. A coarse mesh culinary basket is another useful method because its mesh is wide (¼ inch)—small enough to hold back the seeds, yet large enough to push the pulp through quickly. This is perfect for making ice cream, as you may want a puree that contains chunks of pulp.

A modified Roma tomato sauce processor pulping pawpaws at KSU

Some pawpaw pulpers have had moderate success using a Roma tomato sauce maker to process their fruits at home. This requires modifying a grape spiral attachment by removing the last two spirals to allow the seeds to move through, plus using a salsa screen. You will still want to remove the skin from the fruits before running through the mill. Expect at least a 10% loss of pulp with this method, as plenty of pulp will cling to the seeds. On the plus side, the pulp that comes out is evenly textured and can freeze flat in resealable plastic freezer bags.

When pulping pawpaw fruit, toss out any bruised or discolored parts, as they may add bitterness. Also, be sure there are no small seeds lurking in the final puree. If one gets thrown in a smoothie, you will be in for an unwelcome "cleanse."

Pulp can be further pureed by running it through a food processor until creamy; optionally, it can be strained through a fine mesh sieve for an uber-smooth puree. The drawback of the food processor is that it incorporates a lot of air into the puree, and this hastens oxidative browning.

If you intend to store the pulp or puree in the refrigerator for a few days rather than freezing it right away, cover it tightly with plastic wrap to block out any air that would oxidize the fruit.

Capturing and preserving the exotic flavors of pawpaws is a rewarding art.

Happy pulping!

CHAPTER 7

RECIPES—WHAT DO I DO WITH ALL THIS FRUIT??

Eating a pawpaw is a gustatory delight akin to taking a tropical vacation. While pawpaws are best enjoyed fresh, the rich and custardy texture, sweetness, and complex flavors make it hard to eat more than one at a time.

Before we jump into the many delightful ways to prepare the pawpaw, let's explore the flavor and nutritional nuances of this bountiful fruit.

The Flavor Gamut

The flavor profile of pawpaws is complex and runs the range of sweet and floral in cultivated select fruits to funky and tannic in random wild fruits. Even within a select cultivar, there can be variation depending on climate, region, and harvest timing, much like wine grapes. In short, the quality of the fruit you begin with can play a big role in the recipe's outcome.

Aside from the source of the fruit—cultivated or foraged—the stage of ripeness will also play a major role in flavor profiles. Let's take a popular favorite cultivated variety like Shenandoah as an example; if picked it off the tree just as it was beginning to ripen, the flesh will be firm and predominately sweet with mild flavor profiles. Let it sit on the counter for two days and the flesh will soften a bit, with the flavors becoming richer and more aromatic. Leave it on the counter for four days and the flesh will begin to become mushy and darken, taking on rich notes of coffee and butterscotch. Each stage can be played with.

Let's start with the basics of how to approach eating a fresh pawpaw fruit. Personally, I split pawpaws in half with my thumbs right through the middle, pull apart the two halves, and squeeze up from the bottom like a push pop, slurp up the pulp and seeds, roll the smooth seeds around in my mouth to glean all the custardy goodness, and then spit them out. Yum! Repeat with the other half. A more dignified approach is to cut the fruit with a knife down the middle or lengthwise as best you can around the large seeds and use a spoon to scoop out the pulp, discarding the seeds and skin. At our pawpaw festival, we make tasting samples by slicing pawpaws into one-inch dials, skin and all, so that folks can easily pick them up, peel the thin strip of skin, and pop it in their mouths. This makes it possible to try multiple cultivars before filling up!

Raw versus Cooked

There is a considerable and palatable difference between using pawpaw fruit in its raw state versus cooking it in recipes. The general consensus is with keeping the pawpaw fruit in a raw, uncooked state to fully appreciate its complexities and subtle aromas.[1] That said, heating the pawpaw in an artful way brings out rich aromas and deeper notes that hint at caramel and butterscotch, with distinct tropical fruitiness.

Traditionally, you will see many baked pawpaw recipes, which makes sense for times when freezers were not as abundant as our current times and the need to capture the harvest lent to baking. The challenge is that baking with flour often masks the pawpaw flavor subtleties and can leave only a vague banana-like taste. But there are tricks to working with pawpaw in heated recipes that create very unique and decidedly delicious outcomes, as you will see in the pages to come.

The surefire way to maintain the pawpaw's rich, tropical flavors is to keep it raw in recipes.

---

1 Fresh pawpaws are only in season for a short time, roughly late August to early October, but frozen pulp is available year-round. See Resources for ordering options.

Because the pawpaw's flavors are highly volatile, cooking or baking to pull them out is an art form; done carefully, it can produce exquisite desserts and savory dishes that are distinctly pawpaw. And somewhere in between are the ever-increasing popular pawpaw ferments of beer, meads, and kombucha, which we will explore. And, of course, some pawpaw cocktails!

Pawpaws: The Original Nutrient-Rich Super Fruit

Nutritionally speaking, paw-paws are vitamin-packed antioxidant powerhouses—the original super fruit! Let's take a quick look at how generous, gratifying, and guiltless this super fruit is:

- Pawpaw protein contains all essential amino acids in contents higher than that of apples, bananas, or oranges.
- Full of vital vitamins and minerals, exceeding peaches, grapes and apples. It is exceptionally high in potassium, calcium, vitamin C, niacin, phosphorus, iron, zinc, copper, and magnesium.
- High in antioxidants and unsaturated fatty acids.

PAWPAW RECIPES GUIDELINES

Some general guidelines and ideas for working with pawpaws in recipes follow.

- Add lemon juice or ascorbic acid to the purée to keep the pulp from browning. Seal pulp well and use within 24 hours or freeze.
- Pawpaw purée can be substituted for mashed banana in any recipe, and may still taste like banana.
- Blend complimentary flavors (vanilla, cinnamon, coconut, lemon) sparingly, careful not to mask the pawpaw flavor.
- Custard and pawpaw make tasty partners. The tropical notes of the pawpaw blend well with the egg, vanilla, and sugariness of custard.
- Many recipes suggest mixing pawpaw with flour; doing so will mellow the rich pawpaw flavor.
- The quality of the fruit you start with will affect flavor, from sweet and light to musky and bitter, each which can be used as an advantage.*
- Use low heat. Do not boil or dry as a fruit leather since this distorts the flavor and can lead to tummy ache.
- For first timers trying pawpaws, eat small amounts. Like many foods, some folks are intolerant.
- Tartness can add a balance to pawpaw's sweetness.
- Mix freely with bourbon.

*One of the best pawpaw dishes I have had was a Pawpaw Tart made at star Chef Spike Gjerde's Woodbury Kitchen in Baltimore. I could tell they had used wild pawpaws because of the tannic, bitter notes that were able to survive the baking. It worked beautifully!

Without further ado, here are some lip-smacking ideas. The recipes are listed from raw to heated to fermented.

RECIPES

"Delicious, nutritious and free for the taking." —Earthy Delights

The following recipes are a collection of the best of my pawpaw recipes developed from experimenting, plus favorites created for our pawpaw festivals. There are inspirations from Alan Bergo, known as the "Forager Chef,"[2] and Ellen Zachos, known as the "Backyard Forager."[3] Additional recipe contributions have been made from both my lovely wife and my beautiful mother, as well as by Leigh Scott, a gourmet vegan chef, and Linda Watkins a nutritionist health goddess. Excerpts are included from The Earthy Delights Recipe Blog: Recipes on the Wild Side.[4]

There are a surprising number of pawpaw recipes in circulation. Most are heavy on butter, cream, wheat flour, and refined sugar; while these ingredients do make excellent partners with pawpaw's flavors, they do nothing to prevent heart disease and diabetes. So, to keep in balance, I have focused mainly on healthy and tasty recipes. Don't worry, I still add in some of the good ol' heart stoppers—because, in many ways, they simply cannot be beat!

2 Learn more about Alan Bergo: www.foragerchef.com
3 Learn more about Ellen Zachos: www.backyardforager.com
4 Earthy Delights Recipe Blog: www.earthydelightsblog.com

RAW PAWPAW RECIPES

PAWPAW FRUIT FOOL

Provided by Earthy Delights

Earthy Delights are leaders in offering wild-harvested and hand-crafted foods from small harvesters and growers to a larger audience via their online store. Earthy Delights' recipe blog is full of culinary gems and images. They have been generous to share a sample with all of us! See their links in the Resources appendix to order pawpaw pulp and many other specialty foods to enliven your palate.

INGREDIENTS

- ❑ 1 cup very cold heavy cream
- ❑ 2 Tbsp sugar
- ❑ ⅓ tsp vanilla extract
- ❑ 1 cup pawpaw purée (about 1 medium pawpaw)

METHOD

1. Prepare pawpaw purée.
2. Place the cream into a clean bowl with the sugar (either regular sugar or powdered confectioner's sugar) and the vanilla extract, then whip until stiff enough to hold soft peaks.
3. Gently fold half (½ cup) of the pawpaw purée into the whipped cream until just barely blended.
4. Add the second ½ cup of the pawpaw purée to the mixture, folding just 3 or 4 times. The idea is to leave large, attractive swirls of pawpaw purée throughout the mixture.
5. Carefully spoon into serving dishes and chill until ready to serve.
6. Garnish with fresh mint leaves if desired.

PAWPAW N'ICE CREAM

By Leigh Scott, Olive Thyme Kitchen

This is the vegan and healthy version of pawpaw "ice cream" developed by Leigh Scott specifically for this book! Leigh is a certified chef in Vienna, Virginia, who focuses on nutritious, delicious whole-food, plant-based cuisine.[5]

Yield: Four ½-cup servings

INGREDIENTS

- ❑ 1 large frozen sliced banana (~1 cup)
- ❑ 1 frozen pawpaw (~1 cup pulp), peeled and seeded
- ❑ ¼ cup light coconut milk
- ❑ 1 teaspoon rum (optional, but recommended)
- ❑ Toasted coconut for topping

METHOD

1. Place all ingredients in a food processor[6] and blend until smooth.
2. Eat as soft serve right away or freeze to make a scoopable dessert.
3. Top with toasted coconut.

---

5 Learn more about Leigh Scott: www.OlivetheThymeKitchen.com
6 A food processor should be used; a blender is usually not powerful enough.

"CHEESECAKE" PAWPAW FROZEN BITES

By Linda Watkins

These are raw, dairy-free "Cheesecake" bites by my good friend and health coach extraordinaire Linda Watkins of Baltimore, Maryland. She lent her considerable talents to helping develop healthy pawpaw recipes just for this book! *Thank you, Linda!*

Yield: 36 "bites"

INGREDIENTS

- ❑ ⅓ cup coconut oil, slowly melted
- ❑ 1 lemon, zested and juiced
- ❑ ⅔ cup pawpaw pulp blended or finely chopped
- ❑ ⅔ cup whole fat coconut milk
- ❑ 1⅓ cup raw cashews, ideally soaked 4 hours or more
- ❑ 1 Tbsp agave nectar
- ❑ 3" stripes of parchment paper
- ❑ Mini muffin pans

METHOD

1. Slowly melt the coconut oil to keep it raw (under 118°F).
2. Wash and dry the lemon thoroughly. Zest the lemon before juicing it using a zesting tool or small grate to zest the skin. Set zest aside for garnish.
3. Squeeze the juice from the zested lemon into a bowl; discard seeds.
4. Using a blender, mix all ingredients, except lemon zest, until smooth.
5. Pour into mini muffin tins lined with parchment paper,[7] then sprinkle with lemon zest on top of each bite.
6. Freeze at least 1 hour before removing from the muffin pan and enjoying!

---

7 Chef Linda's Helpful Hint: Lay a 3" strip of parchment paper across the inside of each mini muffin cup, extending outside each cup enough to be able to pull each bite out after freezing. If you don't have parchment paper, the bites can be removed using a butter knife.

RAW AND CHUNKY PAWPAW NECTAR

By Linda Watkins

Yield: 4 cups

INGREDIENTS

- ❏ 1 Tbsp agar agar sea vegetable flakes
- ❏ 1 cup water
- ❏ ⅓ cup melted coconut oil
- ❏ ⅔ cup whole fat coconut milk (or any non-dairy milk)
- ❏ 1⅓ cup soaked raw cashews
- ❏ Juice of 1 lemon
- ❏ 1 Tbsp agave nectar
- ❏ ⅔ cup blended pawpaw pulp
- ❏ ⅔ cup whole pawpaw fruit, coarsely chopped
- ❏ 1 tsp lemon zest

METHOD

1. Bring the agar agar and water to a boil, then simmer 1 minute.
2. Put into a blender with the remaining ingredients except the whole pawpaw and lemon zest.
3. Mix until well blended in blender.
4. Pour into glass bowl, then add the remaining coarsely chopped pawpaw fruit, stirring to incorporate.
5. Sprinkle lemon zest over top.
6. Refrigerate until solidified.

Option: Chill in individual ½-cup servings, then sprinkle zest over each bowl.

Recipe

✗ Long Creek Homestead ✗
Pawpaw Fest Ice Cream

FROM THE KITCHEN OF — Ashley Judd and Carolyn "Maw Maw" Judd

The consensus is that the next best thing to fresh pawpaws is eating them in ice cream. This is largely because the fruit is still in a raw state. This is one of the simplest, yet most flavorful, pawpaw recipes that always creates a long waiting line at our annual pawpaw fest! I think half the people come just for the pawpaw ice cream!

INGREDIENTS:	METHOD: YIELD: 2 Quarts
1 quart Half and Half or 3:1 whole cream/whole milk	1) Using an electric blender, combine all ingredients except the pulp.
1 TBSP vanilla extract	2) Add the pulp in the blender last.
Dash of salt	3) Don't blend all the way so you can end up with some nice fruit chunks.
1/3 to 1/2 cup of simple syrup (optional) [1]	4) Use a two-quart ice cream maker (if you have a one-quart ice cream maker, the recipe can be cut in half).
2½ cups pawpaw pulp	5) After the ice cream maker stops, let it sit for 30 minutes before serving. [2]

NOTES:

[1] The simple syrup is an optional ingredient in the PawPaw Fest Ice Cream. It improves the texture and body of the ice cream, plus it helps lower the freezing point. Usually, no added sugar is needed because of the natural sweetness from the pawpaw pulp, but if you prefer a sweeter outcome, add ½ cup of simple syrup or granulated sugar prior to adding the pulp.

[2] Note that most ice cream maker motors need to cool down completely before being ready to make a second batch. We learned this the hard way during our first pawpaw fest!

HEATED PAWPAW RECIPES

PAWPAW CHEESECAKE

By Alan Bergo, The Forager Chef

Alan Bergo is the keystone between the best of wild flavors and gourmet food. He hunts the most unique flavors the wild has to offer and turns them into exquisite delicacies, and he's a fine cameraman to boot!

My friend—and uncommon fruit guru—Lee Reich[8] turned me onto Alan and the phenomenal pawpaw cheesecake recipe shown below. Lee told me it is a Thanksgiving favorite for his family and that he has been able to store his pawpaws fresh until Thanksgiving in order to make it! When it comes to fruits, Lee is a magician.

Chef Alan's Notes: The pawpaw's fruity flavor makes it a natural thing to enjoy in cheesecake form, as the flavors pair especially well with dairy, and really could be used in anything with a creamy texture, like a pudding, custard, or ice cream. It's also necessary to cut the flavor of the pawpaw a bit as I do here with cheese; when eaten raw, pawpaw can have a slightly bitter note. When working with pawpaws, keep in mind they have a delicate flavor, so simple preparations are the best for them. I would also avoid excess spices, except maybe a bit of ginger or honey if it's a tannic variety. A bit of lemon, too, will give them a lift and help their flavor to shine. Caramel is a great partner, too, but I would avoid chocolate with pawpaw desserts.

The other important thing to know is that the more heat you apply to pawpaw, the less of its perfume will be in the finished product. This is why the pawpaw is added at the end in this recipe, which is different than most pastry cream—which, essentially, is what this is.

This is probably my favorite way to serve pawpaws, and is a recipe I learned by watching my old pastry chef at the legendary Midwestern restaurant, Heartland. Steaming the cheesecake can seem tricky, but once you've gotten the process down, the results are worth the effort, giving the lightest, fluffiest result you've ever had. It's pictured here with a simple sauce made from wild blueberries and a dash of lemon juice, but it's also good all by itself.

If steaming the cheesecake sounds like a lot of work, you can also cook the batter in ramekins to make smaller, individual cheesecakes, which is how we originally served it at the restaurant. Since it's not possible to put a crust in the ramekins, you may want to garnish it with something crunchy, like granola.

---

8 Read Lee Reich's blog: www.leereich.com/blog

Yield: One 8-inch spring form pan, or roughly 12 servings

BLACK WALNUT-GRAHAM CRUST INGREDIENTS

- ❑ 5 tablespoons unsalted butter
- ❑ 1½ cups graham crumbs (roughly 12 crackers)
- ❑ ¼ cup sugar
- ❑ ½ teaspoon fresh ground cinnamon
- ❑ ½ teaspoon salt
- ❑ ½ cup finely chopped black walnuts, or regular walnuts

FILLING INGREDIENTS

- ❑ 2 large eggs + 3 yolks, at room temperature
- ❑ ¾ cup sugar
- ❑ 1 lb. high quality cream cheese
- ❑ 2 cups (1 lb.) pawpaw purée
- ❑ Zest of half a Meyer lemon + 2 tablespoons juice (or substitute fresh lemon juice)

METHOD FOR THE CRUST

1. Preheat the oven to 350°F.
2. Melt the butter, then mix with the graham crumbs, sugar, cinnamon, salt, and the ground walnuts.
3. Press the mixture into an 8-inch spring form pan or square baking dish.
4. Bake for 12-13 minutes, or until lightly browned.
5. Cool the crust while you prepare the filling.

METHOD FOR THE FILLING

1. Beat the whole eggs, yolks and sugar using a stand mixer with the whisk attachment until light and doubled in volume.

2. Meanwhile, purée the cream cheese and the pawpaw purée in a food processor until smooth.

3. Add the pawpaw cheese mixture to the whipped egg mixture and continue mixing with the whisk attachment for 15 minutes.

4. Fold in the lemon juice and zest.

5. Pour into the cooled crust.

6. Bake the cheesecake in a water bath (optional) at 300°F for 70-80 minutes, making sure to check on it regularly at the end.

7. When in doubt, undercook it slightly. The cheesecake needs to be slightly under-baked, and should jiggle gently in the middle.

8. Turn off the oven, and allow the cheesecake to continue cooking, uncovered, until it comes to room temperature.

9. Remove from the oven, then refrigerate until needed, uncovered.[9]

9 Chef Alan's Note: The cheesecake can be baked and frozen, then thawed when ready to serve.

VEGAN LEMON PAWPAW "CHEESE" CAKE WITH OATMEAL PECAN CRUST

By Leigh Scott

Yield: 8

CRUST INGREDIENTS

- ☐ ¾ cup rolled oats
- ☐ ⅓ cup oat flour
- ☐ ⅓ cup raw pecans
- ☐ ¼ cup Grade A maple syrup, amber color
- ☐ 1 tsp vanilla extract
- ☐ Pinch of salt

FILLING INGREDIENTS

- ☐ 2 cups raw cashews
- ☐ 2 cups pawpaw fruit, seeded and mashed
- ☐ 1 Tbsp lemon juice
- ☐ ¼ cup Grade A maple syrup, amber color
- ☐ Pinch of salt
- ☐ 8 ounces coconut milk, well blended
- ☐ 5 tsp agar agar sea vegetable flakes
- ☐ Coconut flakes, toasted

METHOD FOR THE CRUST

1. Preheat the oven to 350 degrees.
2. Add the oats, oat flour, pecans, maple syrup, vanilla extract, and salt to a food processor.
3. Blend for a few minutes until the mixture begins to come together.
4. Press the mixture into a spring form pan and bake at 350°F for about 25 minutes or until light brown.
5. Remove from the oven and let cool while preparing the filling.

METHOD FOR THE FILLING

1. Soak the cashews in hot water for 30 minutes.
2. Drain the cashews well, then put them into a food processor.
3. Add the mashed pawpaw, lemon juice, maple syrup, and salt.
4. Blend well until mixture is smooth and creamy.
5. In a saucepan, add the coconut milk and whisk in the agar agar flakes.
6. Bring the coconut milk mixture to a low boil.
7. Continue whisking and stirring for about 4 minutes, until the agar agar is dissolved.
8. Remove from heat.
9. Add the coconut milk mixture to the cashew mixture.

10. Blend well, then spoon it into the prepared crust.

11. Top with toasted coconut.

12. Chill well until ready to serve.

Recipe

✗ Long Creek Homestead ✗
Pawpaw Jam
Ashley Judd and Michael Judd

FROM THE KITCHEN OF –

I feel like it is time to throw in a simple recipe! One that can use up a lot of pawpaw pulp when the harvest is abundant. The Long Creek Homestead Pawpaw Jam is a favorite at our annual pawpaw fest, where we cook it down on a wood-fired rocket stove. A what? Yes, a rocket stove! The rocket stove is an ingenious appropriate technology that uses very little wood to heat quickly, practically eliminating smoke and hard work.

INGREDIENTS:

Our pawpaw fest jam is simply hand pulped fruits, water, and a little lemon juice, that's it.

4 pounds of fresh pawpaws peeled and seeded

1/2 cup water

Lemon juice to flavor – 1 tbsp

METHOD: YIELD: 10 8oz Jars

Place all ingredients in an uncovered pot and slow cook it over about 20-30 minutes on low to mild heat while stirring. The aromas that come off the jam are exquisite and make the process a real joy. We serve the lumpy and luscious jam on sourdough bread fresh out of the earthen oven. Touch of Appalachian heaven!

NOTES:

This deluxe rocket stove made by InStove makes a great summer kitchen, and can fit a pressure cooker or large wok.

PAWPAW JAM/BUTTER

A more refined recipe for making pawpaw jam, which comes out as a smooth butter, can be taken directly from Kentucky State University's recipe book online[10] or from Friends Drift Inn, also online.[11] I took tips from both recipes, then fashioned my own recipe in the kitchens of Herrington Bay on the Maryland eastern shore, who hosted me not once but twice while writing this book, and generously and boldly let me loose in their kitchen to play with pawpaw recipes. Thank you, Anna and Bob!

There is something very amazing about fresh, warm pawpaw jam. When you cook it down slowly in a thick saucepan, the jam gains a rich aroma reminiscent of brownies and bananas. Throw in some good whiskey and a dash of zest and you're happy trailing on a custard delight from the woods!
Yields: One half gallon

INGREDIENTS

- ❑ Zest and juice from 1 lemon
- ❑ Zest and juice from 1 orange
- ❑ 5 lbs pawpaw pulp
- ❑ 2 cups water
- ❑ ¾ cups sugar
- ❑ ½ cup whiskey or bourbon
- ❑ 2 tsp vanilla
- ❑ 1 tsp salt

METHOD

1. Zest the lemon and orange. Set zest aside.
2. In a food processor, blend the pawpaw pulp with the lemon and orange juices.
3. In a large, thick saucepan, add the pulp mixture to the water. Heat over low to med heat for 10 minutes, stirring often.
4. Remove from the heat.
5. Add sugar, whiskey, and vanilla.
6. Return to low/med heat—be sure not to overheat—stir frequently 30-45 minutes.
7. Remove from heat.
8. Add zest and salt. (Note: If the zest is added during cooking, it will release bitter notes.)

Pawpaw Jam/Butter is thick and spreadable; it has a dark yellow appearance and presents strong flavors of caramel, vanilla, and pawpaw. Pair it with shortbread with berries on top to balance any bitter notes.

---

10 Kentucky State University pawpaw recipes: www.pawpaw.kysu.edu/Recipes.htm
11 Friends Drift Inn recipes can be found at www.friendsdriftinn.com

PAWPAW CURD

Provided by Earthy Delights[12]

Maybe it is from my time growing up in the English midlands scoffing scones laden with thick chunks of butter and tart curds that has me partial to this well- fashioned recipe by Earthy Delights, but as they point out "the sweetness of the pawpaws benefits from a little tartness to give it balance." I concurred.

Fruit curds are a mixture of fruit juice or purée, eggs, sugar and butter – lots and lots of rich, silky butter. Traditionally served at afternoon tea with bread, cakes and pastries, fruit curds make a refreshing alternative to jam or custard.

Creamy, spreadable and eminently edible pawpaw curd

12 Earthy Delights, America's premier supplier of specialty foods to quality-conscious American chefs: www.earthy.com. See the Resources appendix for how to order pawpaw pulp and many other specialty foods to enliven your palate.

It's super easy to create spectacular, fresh-tasting desserts with homemade pawpaw curd. One of our favorite ways to use it is spread on crisp-baked rectangles of puff pastry, topped with a combination of fresh fruit, nuts and berries.

Yield: 4 servings

INGREDIENTS

- ❑ 4 large eggs
- ❑ 1 cup pawpaw purée, strained through a fine mesh sieve
- ❑ ¼ cup lemon juice
- ❑ ⅔ cup sugar
- ❑ ¾ cup (1½ sticks) cold unsalted butter, cut into ½-inch pieces

METHOD

1. Combine the eggs, pawpaw purée, lemon juice, and sugar in a non-reactive mixing bowl or in the top half of a double boiler.
2. Whisk together to combine ingredients.
3. Set the bowl over a pot of gently simmering water or use a double boiler, stirring constantly with a whisk.
4. Stir and scrape along the sides and bottom of the bowl as you go. It's important to keep everything moving, especially around the edges, to avoid the dreaded "scrambled" curd.
5. Continue to cook and stir until the mixture begins to thicken noticeably, 8 to 10 minutes. Don't worry, you'll be able to tell.
6. Remove the bowl from the heat and set it on a doubled kitchen towel on a work surface.
7. Begin whisking in the butter, a piece or two at a time, stirring until each piece is completely incorporated before adding more.
8. Continue adding butter and stirring until all the butter has been used and the consistency is smooth and glossy.
9. Spoon the mixture into a medium bowl.
10. Gently press a sheet of plastic wrap directly onto the surface of the curd and allow to cool at room temperature.
11. Place the cooled curd into the refrigerator to chill for at least an hour before using. The pawpaw curd will continue to thicken up as it cools.[13]

---

13 Tightly sealed in a jar, pawpaw curd keeps for weeks in the refrigerator. For even longer storage, freeze it. Pawpaw curd freezes exceptionally well (must be all that butter!), allowing you to enjoy pawpaws the entire year round.

PAWPAW CRÈME BRÛLÉE

By Ellen Zachos, The Backyard Forager

Ellen Zachos has written seven books, two of which are tops on my list: *Backyard Foraging: 65 Familiar Plants You Didn't Know You Could Eat*, and *The Wildcrafted Cocktail*. Of course, Ellen is a fan of eating and drinking pawpaws (be sure to see her Sugar Bear Cocktail a bit later in this chapter). Ellen has figured life out: she teaches foraging mixology workshops across the U.S. and lectures at botanic gardens, flower shows, and garden clubs around the world—my heroine!

Yield: 6 serving in 3" ramekins

INGREDIENTS

- ❑ 2 large (or 3 small) perfectly ripe pawpaws
- ❑ 2 cups heavy cream
- ❑ 2 T bourbon
- ❑ ⅔ cup sugar plus 6 T for sprinkling
- ❑ ⅛ teaspoon salt

- ❑ 5 egg yolks (save the whites for meringue cookies, or add them to your next omelet or scramble)
- ❑ Six 3-inch ramekins
- ❑ Kitchen torch

METHOD

1. Purée the pawpaws: Slice each pawpaw in half and scoop out the flesh. The seeds are large and the fruit clings tenaciously to the seeds. So as not to waste a precious speck of fruit, use your fingernail to slice through the jacket of pawpaw flesh that coats the seed, then pull it off.

2. Transfer the flesh to the bowl of a food processor then purée it until it's perfectly smooth.[14] Set aside.

3. Combine the cream and bourbon in a saucepan; bring it just barely to a simmer. Whisk to prevent scorching. Remove it from the heat as soon as the first bubbles appear, and set it aside.

4. Preheat the oven to 350°F.

5. In a separate bowl, whisk the sugar and salt into the egg yolks.

6. Add the heated cream mixture to the eggs, a little at a time, whisking constantly to prevent the egg from scrambling. This is called "tempering" the eggs.[15]

7. Stir in the pawpaw purée and combine thoroughly.

8. Divide the custard mixture evenly into the six 3" ramekins.

---

14 Pawpaw purée freezes well, so if you end up with more than a cup, you can freeze the leftovers. Or you can just eat it with a spoon.

15 With tempering, the goal is to raise the temperature of the eggs without cooking them. If you add too much hot liquid too quickly, the eggs will cook and solidify rather than form a silky, thickened liquid. It's easier than it sounds, as long as you proceed slowly and carefully.

9. Place the ramekins in a shallow roasting pan.

10. Fill the pan with water to within a half inch of the top of the ramekins.

11. Bake at 350°F for about 30 minutes. The tops of the custards should not be entirely solid when you take them out of the oven; they should look a little jiggly.

12. Refrigerate the custards at least 6 hours or overnight.

13. Before serving, sprinkle a light layer of sugar on top of each custard (about 1 Tablespoon per ramekin).

14. Using a kitchen torch, brûlée the sugar until desired toasted state.

15. Let it cool (briefly!) to form that glassy, sweet topping that cracks so satisfyingly under a gentle whap from your spoon.

VEGAN PAWPAW MEXICAN LASAGNA WITH BLACK BEANS AND POTATO

By Leigh Scott

Sweet and spicy combination!

Yield: Makes two layered enchiladas, which can each be cut into four wedge-shaped servings

ENCHILADA INGREDIENTS

- ½ small onion, chopped
- 1 large garlic clove, minced
- Approximately ¼ cup of low-sodium vegetable broth
- 2 cups black beans, mashed[16]
- ½ cup brown rice, cooked
- ½ tsp cumin
- ½ tsp coriander
- ¼ tsp chili powder
- ½ tsp unsweetened cocoa powder
- Salt and pepper to taste
- 4 small to medium red or gold potatoes, peeled and cooked
- Approximately ¼ cup of unsweetened almond milk
- 2 pawpaws, peeled, seeded and mashed
- 8 corn tortillas
- Approximately 1¾ cups enchilada sauce (about two 15-oz cans)
- Salsa, if desired
- Avocado, diced, if desired

CASHEW CREAM INGREDIENTS

- ½ cup raw cashews
- ½ cup hot water
- 2 T nutritional yeast
- 1 T lemon juice
- Salt and pepper to taste

METHOD FOR THE "LASAGNA"

1. Preheat oven to 350°F.
2. In a large skillet, cook the onion and garlic in the vegetable broth or water until lightly browned.
3. Add the beans, brown rice, cumin, coriander, chili powder, and cocoa powder.
4. Stir well to combine; season to taste with salt and pepper. Set aside.
5. In a small bowl, mash the potatoes with the unsweetened almond milk until creamy.
6. Season the potatoes to taste with salt and pepper. Set aside.

---

16 Canned beans are fine, as long as you choose beans that have no salt added, as salt added during the first stage of cooking makes the beans less digestible.

7. In another small bowl, ready the mashed pawpaws. Set aside.

8. Place two corn tortillas in a 9"x13" baking dish.

9. Spread approximately ⅛ cup of enchilada sauce on each tortilla.

10. Spread half of the bean mixture on each tortilla.

11. Put a second tortilla on top of the bean mixture, then spread approximately ⅛ cup enchilada sauce on top of each tortilla.

12. Spread half of the mashed potatoes on each tortilla.

13. Put a third tortilla on top of the mashed potatoes and spread with approximately ⅛ cup enchilada sauce on top of each tortilla.

14. Spread half of the mashed pawpaw on each tortilla.

15. Top with the fourth tortilla.

16. Pour the remaining enchilada sauce over the top of the tortillas.

17. Cover the baking dish with aluminum foil.

18. Bake approximately 30 minutes or until heated through.

19. During the baking process, make the cashew cream (see method below).

20. Let sit, covered, on cool working surface about 15 minutes to allow the "lasagna" to meld.

21. Remove the foil.

22. Top the lasagna with the cashew cream, salsa, and avocado, if desired, before serving.

METHOD FOR THE CASHEW CREAM

1. Soak the cashews in ½ cup hot water for about 30 minutes.

2. Combine the cashew mixture, nutritional yeast, and lemon juice in a blender or food processor.

3. Blend until smooth.

4. Add salt and pepper to taste.

5. Add additional hot water, a small amount at a time as needed if the sauce is too thick.

6. Spoon the cashew cream on top of the enchiladas before serving.

VEGAN PAWPAW AND PECAN WHOLE WHEAT PANCAKES WITH CARAMEL SAUCE

By Leigh Scott

Chef Leigh's Notes: It works best to make the caramel sauce first so that it will be ready when the pancakes are hot off the griddle. You will need a candy thermometer to assure the sauce reaches the necessary temperature.

Makes 4 servings

CARAMEL SAUCE INGREDIENTS

- ❑ ½ cup almond milk
- ❑ ½ cup Grade A maple syrup, amber color
- ❑ ¼ tsp salt
- ❑ ½ tsp vanilla extract

PANCAKE INGREDIENTS

- ❑ 1⅓ cups whole wheat pastry flour (do *not* use regular whole wheat flour; it would be too heavy)
- ❑ 4 tsp baking powder
- ❑ ½ tsp salt
- ❑ 1⅓ cup oat milk (you can substitute another non-dairy milk, but oat milk is best because it encourages browning)
- ❑ 3-4 pawpaws – peeled, seeded and mashed
- ❑ 1 tsp vanilla extract
- ❑ ¼ cup chopped pecans (toasted, if desired)

METHOD FOR THE CARAMEL SAUCE

1. Combine the almond milk and maple syrup in a heavy saucepan.
2. Whisk constantly until mixture comes to a full boil and the mixture reaches 235˚.
3. Continue to whisk the boiling sauce for 8 minutes.
4. Remove from the heat.
5. Stir in the salt and vanilla extract.
6. Spoon over warm pancakes and enjoy!
7. Store any leftover caramel sauce in the refrigerator.

METHOD FOR THE PANCAKES:

1. Once the caramel has been made, combine the flour, baking powder, and salt in a bowl. Whisk to mix.
2. In a separate bowl, combine the oat milk, mashed pawpaw, and vanilla extract.
3. Use a spoon to make a well in the flour mixture, then add the almond milk mixture and stir until just combined. Do not overmix. Add more oat milk, if needed, to reach the right consistency.
4. Using a ½-cup measuring cup, pour batter onto a hot, non-stick skillet, forming pancakes.
5. Turn the pancakes when the tops begin to dry and the bottoms turn light brown.
6. Remove from the pan when the second side turns light brown.
7. To serve, sprinkle with chopped pecans and drizzle with caramel sauce, if desired.

PAWPAW PANNA COTTA

By Alan Bergo

I like the panna cotta with a little bit of sharp berry sauce or citrus to wake it up a bit, just think of garnishes that would taste good with a banana. Pictured is wild plum jam thinned with a dash of orange and lemon juice to make a sauce, along with toasted hickory nuts to add crunch.

Yield: Six 4-ounce ramekins

INGREDIENTS

- ❑ ½ cup sugar
- ❑ 2 cups heavy cream
- ❑ 3 sheets leaf gelatin or 3.5 teaspoons powdered gelatin
- ❑ 6 oz (⅔ cup) frozen or fresh pawpaw purée
- ❑ Dash of fresh Meyer lemon, or lemon
  juice, to taste
- ❑ A few scrapes of orange zest

METHOD

1. Gently warm the cream and sugar, whisking until the sugar is melted.
2. Meanwhile, bloom the gelatin until soft in ice water, then squeeze the water out. (If using powdered gelatin, add it directly to the warm cream and sugar, then whisk).
3. Puree the warm cream mixture with the pawpaw purée and the gelatin.
4. Pass through a strainer (optional).
5. Zest the lemon into its own dish.
6. Add the lemon juice and the zest to taste.
7. Check the seasoning and adjust as needed (you should taste a hint of citrus in the background).
8. Ladle the mixture into 4-ounce ramekins
9. Refrigerate overnight until the panna cotta is set.

COCKTAILS

FROZEN PAWPAW MARGARITA

By Chef Rosie Moot

My good friend and fellow pawpaw aficionado, David Doyle, connected me with his cousin—Chef Rosie Moot of Pico Taqueria in Chincoteague, Virginia. Chef Rosie makes this outstanding frozen pawpaw margarita. This connection has changed my life! Muchisimas Gracias!

- ❑ 1 shot lime juice
- ❑ 1 shot pawpaw puree
- ❑ ½ shot simple syrup
- ❑ 1½ shot tequila
- ❑ ½ shot Deep Eddy Peach
- ❑ 10 ice cubes

PAWPAW PINA COLADA

Brought to you by the Judds

We had a pawpaw piña colada party once to work out a recipe . . . but it was so much fun, we forgot to write anything down ☺

The gist was throwing the following ingredients in a blender. The beauty of this recipe is you can adjust the measurements of each of the ingredients to suit your own personal taste. The high nutrient value of this concoction kept the party going long into the night!

INGREDIENTS

- ❑ Pawpaw pulp
- ❑ Coconut milk
- ❑ Pure pineapple juice

- ❑ Flor de Cana dark rum
- ❑ Wee bit of vanilla

SUGAR BEAR COCKTAIL RECIPE[17]

By Ellen Zachos

On a more refined cocktail note . . . Ellen Zachos, the Backyard Forager, celebrates the love story between pawpaw and bourbon in style with the Sugar Bear Cocktail.

INGREDIENTS

- ❑ 2 ounces bourbon
- ❑ 4 ounces pawpaw purée
- ❑ ½ ounce acorn orgeat

- ❑ ½ teaspoon verjuice
- ❑ Ground dried spicebush berries (optional)

METHOD

Combine the bourbon, pawpaw purée, acorn orgeat, and verjuice in a shaker with ice and shake for 30 seconds. Pause, then shake again for 30 seconds. Pawpaw purée is thick and extra shaking is required to mix it up. A sprinkling of ground spicebush berries is a tasty and attractive garnish.

---

17 Excerpted from *The Wildcrafted Cocktail*© by Ellen Zachos. Used with permission from Storey Publishing.

SPECIAL MENTION: PAWPAW MOONSHINE

Pawpaw makes a fine moonshine.[18] Known as the "hillbilly banana" to some, pawpaw moonshine has long been added into corn mash for a flavorful white lighting.

Pawpaw moonshine also makes a mighty fine brandy. Kelly Sauber, the distiller at Fifth Element Spirits in Ohio[19], makes a much sought-after pawpaw brandy. Kelly was the first to brew a pawpaw beer for the Ohio Pawpaw Festival way back in 2002. The festival now boasts nine pawpaw flavored brews from eight Ohio breweries (see the next section on ferments).

---

18 Appalachian Distillery makes a 100% West Virginian pawpaw moonshine, visit them at appalachian-moonshine.com.
19 Learn more about Kelly Sauber and Fifth Element Spirits: http://www.westendciderhouse.com/fifth-element-spirits.html

PAWPAW CINNAMON MEAD

By Elisha and Elizabeth Somerville

Pawpaw mead[20] is one of the best honey wines I have ever tasted—which is saying something! Mead is made with honey as the main ferment to which fruit and herbs can be added. The aromas and subtle pawpaw flavors pair beautifully with the full body base of honey. It can be enjoyed as a dessert wine or poured over ice to lighten it up as a summer drink.

Our good friends and herbal wizards Elisha and Elizabeth Somerville took about 40 pounds of our pawpaws to run multiple mead variations and came back with some mighty fine wine and testing notes. The winner of various batches is their Pawpaw Cinnamon Mead . . . it is purely nectarous!
Yield: 5 gallons

INGREDIENTS

- ❏ 1 packet Lalvin D-47 yeast
- ❏ Filtered non-chlorinated water
- ❏ 10 cups pawpaw pulp

- ❏ 5 quarts raw wildflower honey
- ❏ 3 tablespoons cinnamon chips

METHOD

1. Prepare yeast: add packet of yeast to a little warm water. Let it sit for approximately 15 minutes.
2. Meanwhile, place pawpaw pulp and 2 quarts of the honey into a large jar or crock.
3. After 15 minutes has passed, add the yeast mixture and approximately 1 gallon of filtered water to the brew and stir vigorously.
4. Cover with a cloth and leave for 1 to 2 days, stirring 2 to 4 times per day. This type of open fermentation allows the yeast to get a good start, but is not ideal for the entirety of the process.
5. After 1 to 2 days in the cloth-covered jar or crock, pour the brew into a 5-gallon carboy[21] with an air lock and keep in a dark place at room temperature.
6. Check the brew weekly, adding a quart of honey with a little water every week for 3 weeks in a row. The timing doesn't have to be exact as to when the honey is added, and you can add more or less to your taste. When all is said and done, you want to have a full carboy and will want to have added the 3 remaining cups of honey before the brewing process is finished.

---

20 A recommended must-read for any mead maker is Jereme Zimmerman's *Make Mead Like a Viking* because it's so freeing in philosophy and encourages you to let your imagination guide your recipes.
21 A carboy is a large glass bottle used in the winemaking process. These can be purchased online from winemaking companies and other distributors.

7. You will know that it is finished when you no longer see the air lock bubbling. Expect this to take at least a month.

8. When the fermentation is finished, siphon off all of the clear mead into bottles with airtight lids. You can expect to have a heavy layer of dregs at the bottom of the carboy that you don't want in your bottled mead, so it's ok to take the time to let everything settle for a bit before bottling. Wine bottles with corks, beer bottles with crimped lids, or glass bottles with swing-top clasps work well for bottling your mead.

9. Store the bottled mead in a cool, dark location. This brew is great to drink as soon as you bottle it, but also gets better with age. *Cheers!*

PAWPAW FERMENTS: BEER, MEAD, AND KOMBUCHA

Pawpaw is making headlines in popular culture thanks very much to its success as a tasty beer. The Ohio Pawpaw Festival and its founder, Chris Chmiel, have fermented a small revolution in the micro-brewery world Indeed, it seems the pawpaw beers have become the keystone to the festival, which now includes at least eight different breweries and a brewer's round table event to share the wonders of pawpaw and fermenting.

I am going to dodge the rabbit hole of beer and pawpaws and just put in a few collected notes here as, fortunately, there are some very good articles posted online that delve into the intricacies of the brewing process.

If you're really thirsty to learn more, then plan to hit up the Ohio Pawpaw Festival![22]

2018 OHIO PAWPAW FESTIVAL BEER LINEUP

The beer line up for the Ohio Pawpaw Festival in 2018 showcased the diversity of styles that pair well with pawpaw:

- Pawpaw Wheat, Jackie O's Brewery, Athens
- Weasel Pawpaw Pale Ale, Weasel Boy Brewing
- Paw Paw Wa Wa Blonde, North High Brewing
- Pawpaw Hef, Sixth Sense Brewing
- Pawpaw Murkshake IPA, Sixth Sense Brewing
- Pawpaw Weizen, Little Fish Brewing
- PawPale Ale, Devil's Kettle Brewing
- Pawpaw Cream Ale, Maple Lawn Brewery
- Saison Paw Paw, Thirsty Dog Brewing

It seems the pawpaw flavor and aromas come out well in a diversity of styles, with lighter wheat and pale ales making the most headlines.

---

22 Learn more about the Ohio Pawpaw Festival: www.ohiopawpawfest.com

Recipe

✗ Long Creek Homestead ✗
Kombucha
Ron White

FROM THE KITCHEN OF -

Kombucha is a fermented tea made from using green or black tea and a symbiotic culture of yeast and beneficial bacteria known as a SCOBY (Symbiotic Culture Of Bacteria and Yeast), often referred to as the "mother." It makes a tasty, lightly effervescent beverage popular in the health world [1]. I am not typically drawn to kombucha, but when our friend Ron White brought over a batch of homemade pawpaw kombucha, I converted quickly. The clear bottles were filled with a light golden nectar that popped and sizzled. Needless to say, it became an instant new homestead favorite!

INGREDIENTS:	METHOD: YIELD: 1 Quart
A SCOBY	"I start with tea, sugar, and well water. When the fermentation is done, then I bottle it. At that point, I add flavorings. My favorite is one teaspoon of pawpaw pulp added to a 16-ounce bottle. Let it sit until it has carbonated and then enjoy."
Tea (2 tsp of green or black tea per quart of water)	
Well Water – 32oz	
Sugar – required for the SCOBY in fermentation	–Ron White
2 tsp of pawpaw pulp (1 tsp per 16oz of water)	

NOTES:

[1] It has been noted that making it at home can be dodgy if over-fermented, and it can become contaminated, so do your research first! Kombucha has amazing health benefits: the probiotic bacteria provides a boost to gut health; studies show kombucha helps prevent the growth of cancer cells; the fermentation process helps kill bacteria and can be instrumental in fighting infections; and some studies show kombucha can aid with health challenges, such as heart disease, liver ailments, diabetes, and weight loss.

[2] To learn all about the kombucha-making process and acquire a SCOBY, visit the fine folks at Cultures for Health: www.culturesforhealth.com

Pawpaw Food Safety

As with any food, there are a portion of people who have unfavorable reactions with eating pawpaws. These symptoms range from nausea and puffy lips to a rushed trip to the bathroom, but to date, there are no recorded fatalities from eating pawpaws. Heck, even the FDA says they are safe to consume!

Some tissues of the pawpaw, including the bark, leaves, and seeds, contain a variety of alkaloids, phenolic acids, proanthocyanidins, tannins, flavinoids, and acetogenins. While these chemicals can cause allergic reactions, some of them are anticarcenogens, while others have natural or botanical pesticide qualities.

Pawpaw trees and, to a lesser degree, pawpaw fruits, contain medical compounds known as acetogenins. Research on pawpaw acetogenins is showing very promising results for fighting cancer. Acetogenic compounds are found most strongly in the pawpaw's bark, branches, and leaves, and to a lesser degree in the fruits. One might think of it as a mild wild medicinal.

ALL THINGS PAWPAW

For more recipes and additional information on pawpaws, visit our Facebook page, *For the Love of PawPaws*: www.facebook.com/fortheloveofpawpaws. Also see the Resources appendix for an amazing amount of information on all things pawpaw!

FOOD FOR THOUGHT BY R. NEAL PETERSON

"Due to its potential for allergic reaction causing contact dermatitis and possible presence of pesticides, pawpaw consumption may be harmful to humans."*

Because of that statement, a question has arisen about the safety of eating pawpaws. According to the FDA: "The pawpaw has a long history of food use; the FDA does not currently have any evidence that pawpaw is unsafe to eat."**

Indeed, some people are allergic to pawpaw. This is not exceptional, however. Food allergies are many, the most common being milk, eggs, fish, shellfish, tree nuts, peanuts, wheat, and soybeans. Among fruits, the common allergens are apple, peach, and kiwi. This list puts pawpaw allergy in perspective. Pawpaws are not unusual; and the same caution should be exercised in eating them as in eating other fruits.

The statement that pesticides are present in pawpaw seems peculiar. Pesticides are not being sprayed on the fruit—never in the wild, and almost never in cultivation. This claim seems to be a poorly chosen wording, based on the fact that pawpaw—and other plants in the Annona family—contain acetogenins, a class of potent compounds that contain pesticide properties.

We should not be surprised that plants contain toxic compounds, as these are the plant's defense against predation by insects, fungi, and animals. The food plants eaten around the world are full of bioactive compounds. Notable toxic compounds are found in some very popular plants consumed, unknowingly and without concern, each day: potatoes, tomatoes, and eggplant contain acetylcholinesterase inhibitors; tannins are found in tea, coffee, and cocoa; and cabbage, broccoli, and Brussels sprouts contain glucosinolates.

Moderation in eating pawpaw is the sensible approach. Consumption of one or two fresh fruits a day, in season, is normal; it is how humans have consumed them throughout the ages. Daily consumption throughout the year, particularly of a tea brewed from the leaves, is probably unwise.

*wikipedia.org/wiki/Asimina_triloba#Fruits
**Communication to Dr. Kirk Pomper, Kentucky State University

PAWPAWS AND PERMACULTURE

What is Permaculture?

Permaculture is an approach to designing our landscapes based on the successful relationships we see in healthy ecosystems. First, we observe how natural patterns are working together to make a whole system thrive. We then take the outline of these patterns and apply them to our landscapes and lives to create largely self-functioning and productive systems (plantings).

That's permaculture in a nutshell. Now, let's break it down into projects that relate to growing pawpaws.

Swales on Contour

A popular permaculture technique that has proven hugely effective, especially with the pawpaw, is the swale on contour: the ultimate raised bed that passively harvests water. Swales on contour create the conditions pawpaws love, which are on banks that have good drainage near ample water. I have seen dramatic growth differences in pawpaw trees planted on swale berms compared to those planted nearby in flat ground.

Swales on contour are marked out level, perpendicular to the slope, so that sheeting water slows and sinks in. The swale-building process is discussed in detail in my book, *Edible Landscaping with a Permaculture Twist*,[1] so I will simply outline the idea here.

Swales on contour make beautiful sinuous flowing beds that just naturally fit the landscape while passively harvesting rain water.

---

1 *Edible Landscaping with a Permaculture Twist* is available at www.ecologiadesign.com. This book provides step-by-step processes for setting up a diverse and low-maintenance edible landscape for pawpaws and other fabulous uncommon fruits, plus details how to establish food forests, swales, hügelkultur, and much more.

Contour of slope can easily be found using a simple A-frame level (which takes about 10 minutes to construct from scrap wood) or a transit level. A basin is then dug and the soil mounded on the downhill side, creating a berm. Depending on the design, the basin can then be filled with wood chips, mulched with straw, or left to grow as grass and becomes a path alongside the berm. Since the basin is perfectly level along the slope, incoming water stops and sinks into the ground water, effectively harvesting and holding moisture in the root zone. Passive water harvesting with swales on contour, in combination with groundcover plants, a.k.a. living mulch, will keep your landscape verdant and productive even during dry periods. Design to recline!

Small-scale swales with moderate incoming water can fit easily into most landscapes. Be mindful of two things: do not to raise the berm too high, as this can subject it to drying winds, and remember that swales on contour are harvesting water into the water table for quite a distance past the berm; to avoid flooding, don't build them just above your house!

Food Forest Model

Food forests are not about growing food *in* the forest, but, rather, *like* the forest. When we look at healthy forests, we see a lot going on—overstory trees, midstory trees, understory trees, shrubs, groundcovers, vines—all working as a powerful and productive collective. If we take the observations of these successful symbiotic patterns and transfer them to our landscape planning, we are starting with nature's most dynamic design: wisdom.

So, instead of just sticking your fruit tree in a sea of grass with a dinky mulch ring, you design a mini ecosystem for your pawpaw tree planting. You design a "guild" of companions to support its needs and set the stage for successful growth and production that is not reliant on our constant inputs.

I like to break the larger food forest concept down into "patches" to simplify the approach.

The first ingredient in building this mini food forest patch is good soil and moisture retention that support fungi; in turn, these fungi build healthy soils. In Chapter 4 in the Planned Planting section, I cover sheet mulching and deep mulching of woodchips to start soil building and draw in the fungi. Remember, it's all about the fungi!

Once your soil building is in place and you are ready to plant, consider designing in the young fruit tree plant guilds. See Chapter 5: Eco-logical Tree Care, for more information on companion plants.

Two well-spaced sheet-mulched food forest patches for a pair of pawpaws and companion plants.

FOOD FOREST MODEL

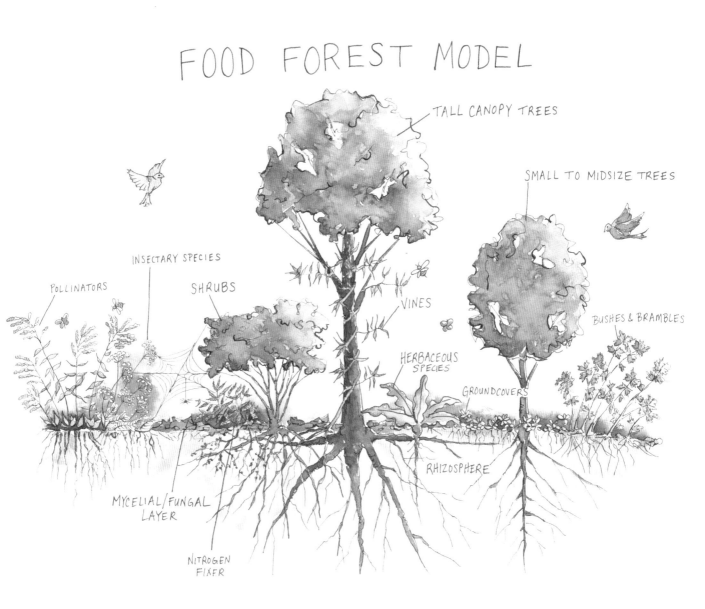

TALL CANOPY TREES

SMALL TO MIDSIZE TREES

INSECTARY SPECIES

POLLINATORS

SHRUBS

VINES

BUSHES & BRAMBLES

HERBACEOUS SPECIES

GROUNDCOVERS

RHIZOSPHERE

MYCELIAL/FUNGAL LAYER

NITROGEN FIXER

A food forest on your landscape can be any as small as 10' x 10' or as large as you'd like to make it, as well as any shape that fits the space or aesthetic.

AGROFORESTRY

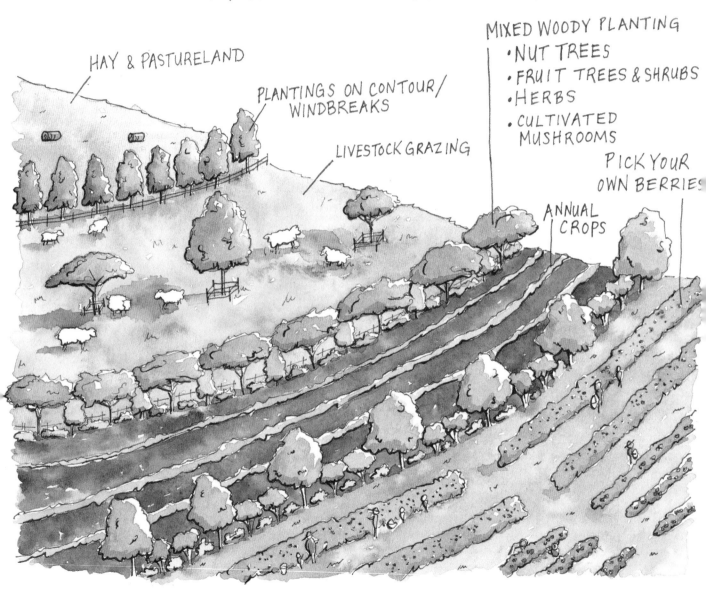

MIXED WOODY PLANTING
- NUT TREES
- FRUIT TREES & SHRUBS
- HERBS
- CULTIVATED MUSHROOMS

PICK YOUR OWN BERRIES

HAY & PASTURELAND

PLANTINGS ON CONTOUR/ WINDBREAKS

LIVESTOCK GRAZING

ANNUAL CROPS

Beyond the Patch: Pawpaws in Agroforestry

For those with space and market interest in growing pawpaws, agroforestry models are the way to go. Agroforestry incorporates woody perennials (trees, shrubs, etc.) with field crops and/or animals. With agroforestry, you get to stack enterprises for diverse harvests and ecological benefits.

Pawpaws stack well into an agroforestry model—especially with animals—since the trees are not palatable to grazing animals . . . even goats! Chris Chmiel, a "pawpaw elder" and permaculture practitioner, combines an extensive pawpaw orchard in Athens, Ohio, with his flock of goats. The chemical *Annonaceous acetogenins*[2] found in the pawpaws leaves, twigs, and bark make them a rare candidate for browsers. Chris notes that the goats help keep the pawpaw understory free of competing growth and donate natural fertility that also helps draw in the pawpaw's main pollinator, the glorious fly. Chris and his wife, Michelle Gorman, operate Integration Acres, which offers commercially available pawpaw pulp, vinaigrette, chutneys, and goat milk cheeses. Integration Acres also incorporates other non-timber forest products, including cultivated mushrooms, ginseng, goldenseal, and spicebush, with pawpaws in adjacent areas not frequented by goats.

Chris also works with improving native pawpaw stands surrounding their homestead by clearing around productive trees that yield chop and drop mulch, mushroom wood, and select wild varieties. Chris points out that working with existing stands can jumpstart production and sales, whereas a pawpaw orchard can take six plus years to begin harvesting. Chris was awarded a grant from Sustainable Agriculture Research & Education (SARE) to research "Increasing Production in Native Stands of Pawpaws."[3]

Another fine agroforestry model that incorporates the pawpaw is exemplified by Red Fern Farm in southeastern Iowa. Tom Wahl and Kathy Dice have successfully mixed the pawpaw into a diverse you-pick agroforestry system that interplants chestnuts, hazelnuts, persimmons, cornelian cherries (fruiting dogwood), heartnuts, and aronia (black chokeberry).

See Resources appendix for contact information for Integration Acres and Red Fern Farm.

---

2 To read what National Institute of Health (NIH) says about Annonaceous acetogenins, visit www.cancer.gov/publications/dictionaries/cancer-drug/def/annonaceous-acetogenins.

3 The final report can be viewed online: https://projects.sare.org/project-reports/fnc00-315/.

Hügelkultur Beds

I would be errant to not mention hügelkultur beds and pawpaws! Hügelkultur is an old Germanic word basically meaning wood covered with soil and mound culture. It is what happens naturally in an old forest where trees have fallen and decades of leaves have covered the wood, inviting the fungi in to munch it all down into rich compost. These hügelkultur mounds can be created on our landscapes in a variety of scales to build long-term fertility and moisture retention. The moist environment of the soil-covered wood draws in fungi to begin the composting process, which ultimately releases nutrients and holds moisture for plantings. Typically, hügelkultur beds are planted with cane fruits (such as raspberries) or fruiting shrubs that can handle the shifting that takes place over the years of breakdown. I have found a sweet spot, however: in the hügel design for pawpaws, of course! When a hügelkultur bed is built and the soil is dumped over top of the wood, a certain amount of the soil naturally cascades down to the base, which makes a nice deep, loose planting soil. This is a happy place for pawpaws, as they gain the benefits of the hügelkultur water harvest and eventual nutrient release.

For more detailed information on creating hugelkultur beds, see my book, Edible Landscaping with a Permaculture Twist, which devotes an entire chapter to the subject.

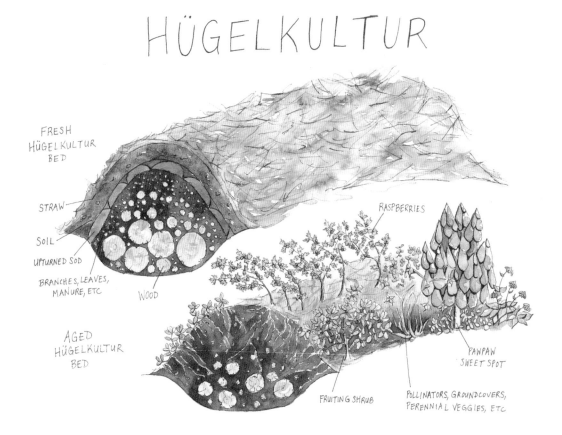

HÜGELKULTUR

FRESH HÜGELKULTUR BED

STRAW

SOIL

UPTURNED SOD

BRANCHES, LEAVES, MANURE, ETC

WOOD

RASPBERRIES

AGED HÜGELKULTUR BED

FRUITING SHRUB

POLLINATORS, GROUNDCOVERS, PERENNIAL VEGGIES, ETC

PAWPAW SWEET SPOT

Building up wood in the hugelkultur bed

Voila! Hugelkultur bed covered!

Greywater Berms

Greywater berms are also a perfect place to plant pawpaw trees since they are basically built-in passive irrigation. Greywater is the used water coming from your sinks, shower, and washing machine that gets gravity-fed or pumped out to shallow troughs in the landscape.[4] The greywater troughs at our home are 2-feet wide by 20-feet long and only a few inches deep; and they are bermed on either side, with contoured planting beds. As long as you are using eco-groovy soaps and cleaners, the raised beds on either side of the trough basically become sub-irrigated beds. Our greywater berms are planted with black currants, gooseberries, and pawpaws.[5]

Greywater trough with raised beds on either side reuses precious water and nutrients

Landscape Planting Ideas

From stunning fruit-tree lined driveways to front yard specimens to edible woodland gardens, the pawpaw highlights landscapes with dense tropical foliage, attractive growth form, and low-hanging fruit. A few ideas for adding pawpaws to the landscape follow. Pawpaw trees graft well with:

- City lots (resilient tree)
- Townhome yards (close spacing)
- Suburban lawns (island and foundation plantings)
- Under power lines (limited height)
- Businesses and urban areas (specimen trees)
- Adjacent to drainage ditches (self-watering)
- Rain gardens (stacking functions)
- Along driveways and parking areas (using microclimates)
- Edible woodland gardens[6] (shade tolerant)
- In swales (contour planting)

---

4 Regular house plumbing or individual appliances, such as a washing machine, can be easily retrofitted into greywater systems, thereby putting your wash water to good use! For more info on greywater systems, check out greywateraction.org.

5 Greywater beds can be extra helpful to pawpaw plantings in regions that are typically too dry for the lush *Asimina tribola*.

6 I designed an edible woodland garden at Top Chef Bryan Voltaggio's Volt restaurant in Frederick, Maryland, that highlights a pair of pawpaw trees mixed in with currants, ginseng, sweet woodruff, fiddlehead ferns, spicebush, and mushroom logs, along with a few other plants. The pawpaws were positioned so their deep green lush foliage can be marveled at by diners sitting in the alcove dining room eating pawpaw tarts—touché!

PAWPAW RAIN GARDENS

Mid- to large-sized rain gardens that have transition zones with a balance of good drainage and access to deep moisture are sweet spots for pawpaws and other favorite edible all-stars. The "Pawpaws in Rain Gardens" illustration shows a sample of working with the different depths and moisture levels found in most rain gardens. In the mid-sized rain garden, we depict the center/wet zone planted with juneberry (*Amelanchier sp.*); the middle/mesic planted with pawpaws ringed around the juneberry; and the transitional zone with blueberries ringing around the pawpaws.

For a larger rain garden space or for a large island planting, I recommend placing an American persimmon in the center, then a ring of pawpaws intermixed with spicebush and aronia, followed by an outer ring of black currants. An added bonus to the cornucopia of fruit this design brings is mixing the golden autumn foliage of the pawpaws and spicebush with the reds of the aronia and persimmon.

For permaculture resource information, please see the Resources appendix.

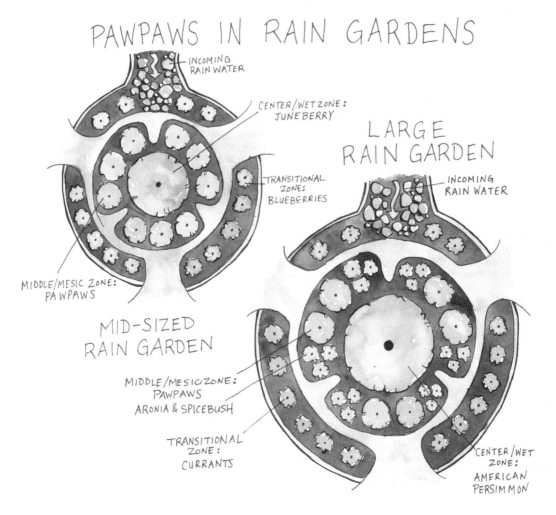

PAWPAWS IN RAIN GARDENS

INCOMING RAIN WATER

CENTER/WET ZONE: JUNEBERRY

LARGE RAIN GARDEN

INCOMING RAIN WATER

TRANSITIONAL ZONE: BLUEBERRIES

MIDDLE/MESIC ZONE: PAWPAWS

MID-SIZED RAIN GARDEN

MIDDLE/MESIC ZONE: PAWPAWS ARONIA & SPICEBUSH

TRANSITIONAL ZONE: CURRANTS

CENTER/WET ZONE: AMERICAN PERSIMMON

COMMERCIAL GROWING AND MARKETING

Pawpaw are a niche market just waiting to be explored.

This appendix is a collection of notes, experiences, and ideas. For more detailed and ongoing research into commercial realities with pawpaws, I default to Kentucky State University's pawpaw program, as its work largely focuses on the pawpaw's potential as a viable commercial crop. See Chapter 2 for additional information on the Kentucky State University's program.

For me, the verdict is out on if pawpaws can become a large-scale commercial enterprise. On the one hand, I see them as a connected part of diverse ecosystems, while also recognizing they are a super adaptive species that have shown strong growth and production in monoculture conditions. I think there is a sweet spot that honors both in agroforestry and market garden designs. They are a super sweet spot for creameries and other value-added product-oriented companies wanting to diversify their variety of flavors.

And then, of course, there is beer. The micro-brewery market is blowing up the pawpaw's popularity and creating a high demand for bulk fruit. Breweries can stack growing pawpaws into their hop production. Harvest inputs are minimal since fruit for ferment does not need to be handpicked or blemish free. Same goes for kombucha companies and vegan product markets.

Deep Run Pawpaw Orchard

My experience with growing pawpaws commercially, mainly, is through my good friend Jim Davis of Deep Run Pawpaw Orchard, located near Westminster, Maryland. Jim's 20+-year enterprise of commercially growing pawpaws has been pioneer and unparalleled. It is one of the main inspirations for creating this manual.

Jim jumped into pawpaw orcharding with both feet back in 1995 by planting hundreds of grafted pawpaw trees on 6.5 acres of an open rolling hilltop adjacent to his home. He has met much success, and also challenges, growing pawpaws commercially over these years with the world's first and largest pawpaw orchard. Jim's early inspirations and encouragement came from his friend Neal Peterson, a.k.a. *Mahatma Pawpaw*, and his drive to pioneer an unexplored adventure. (Learn more about Neal in Chapter 2.)

Jim's friendship with Neal has had many positive influences and affects, starting with the access and ability to work with the best pawpaw seeds and cultivars available. Original plant material was purchased from Northwood Nursery in Oregon. Deep Run's pawpaw orchard is a mix of the following cultivars (percentages are approximated): Shenandoah, 40%; Susquehanna, 20%; Potomac, 5%; Wabash, 5%; Overleese, 5%; Alleghany, 20%; and PA Golden, 5%. These trees are spaced 8 feet apart within rows with 15 feet between rows.

Deep Run Pawpaw Orchard is not your typical pawpaw growing site (i.e., moist, humid, and protected); rather, it is set on the top of hill in full sun. Fortunately, the property is well surrounded by woods that offer some wind protection and insect diversity to help maintain moisture needs and good pollination. In addition, Jim has a good well and extensive drip irrigation system that is a back-up for the annual average rainfall for his region, which is approximately 43" per year. Jim does not use herbicides or insecticides, but does use conventional fertilizer.

While Jim is a lover of wildlife, especially wild fowl, his exclusion of herbicides and insecticides is also practical based. He points out that use of an herbicide around the base of pawpaw trees can be easily absorbed by the trees suckers and drawn into the tree itself, essentially poisoning the tree. Since pawpaws on a commercial scale rely heavily on natural pollination, it would be nonsensical to spray insecticides, thus killing off the helpful pol-

Jim Davis, the pioneer pawpaw orchardist

linators; this applies even to "natural" concentrates such as neem oil, which can have broad-spectrum effects, including harm to bee hives.

Jim largely operates this significant enterprise with only his wife, Donna; he relies on a handful of friends around harvest time. Both Jim and Donna have held other full-time jobs during the many years of running the orchard—which Jim's calls a "serious hobby"—and take time off from their regular positions during harvest season each year. The ability to work other jobs, the isolation of their orchard, and the value of peace of mind have been factors in Jim and Donna's choice to remain a wholesale business.

Deep Run's annual harvest averages around three tons of fruit—over 6,000 pounds! Approximately two-thirds of the harvest is sold as premium-quality fruit; the other third is sold to the beer-making industry. All fruit that is sold as premium quality is carefully handpicked, never touching the ground or being bruised. Hand-picking fruit is an art that requires real dedication. It consumes the Davis' life for a full month during the harvest season, which mainly happens in September.

Jim's goal is to get all handpicked fruit cooled as quickly as possible and shipped within 48 hours of harvest. To accommodate this need, he built a basic 30' x 40' metal storage and processing building with a

20' x 10' walk-in cooler. All premium fruit is hand collected by experienced pawpaw harvesters, carefully laid into bins in single layers to avoid bruising, and carted to the processing building on the back of a small utility vehicle. The cooler is outfitted with an air filter to help draw out the excess ethylene gas produced by the ripening pawpaws.

Most of the Deep Run Orchard's pawpaw fruits are packaged in single layers in flat boxes lined with large bubble wrap on both the top and bottom of the box (with the bubbles facing down for added protection against bruising) for shipping. Each box averages about 18 pounds and is shipped via 2-day express service.[1]

Jim's market for prime fruit is a mix of specialty restaurants and gourmet food stores in New York City, regional pawpaw festivals, farmer market vendors, and online specialty food distributors. Fallen fruit and "seconds" are primarily sold to regional breweries. The wholesale price for premium fruit is around $4.00 per pound and $1.50 for seconds. Selling wholesale fruit, Jim says, brings in approximately $18,000 in profit each year. He recognizes that if they engaged in retail or processing markets, their profit margin would greatly increase, but so would their labor.[2]

Jim notes that the commercial interest in pawpaw orcharding has grown quickly in recent years and he is often contacted by excited, yet naïve, would-be growers. He cautions against jumping in too fast; rather, Jim encourages potential pawpaw growers to research the nuances and time inputs needed to manage a pawpaw orchard, as this is necessary for optimal success. In general, he encourages people to throttle back.

Challenges exist every year that can affect harvest: weather often is the biggest factor, but also fungal spots on the fruit skin that can crack and ruin fruit; high temperatures around harvest time that

1 To order from Deep Run Orchard, please contact Jim Davis by email (djim4265@aol.com) or phone (410-848-9826).
2 With direct retail, nursery plant and hybrid seed sales, a commercial orchard like Deep Run could potentially average four times the profit margin earned from only wholesaling the fruit. A value-added business that processes the fruit into pulp and then into a niche market product like gelato would further capitalize on a pawpaw orchard this scale, and potentially make good income, but then that would be your life.

quicken ripening and cannot be picked quickly enough; and strong winds and storms can drop a lot of unripened fruit. Jim doesn't know from year to year how the dice will roll out.

For marketing purposes, Jim points out that purchaser/consumer education is key. Educating on how to handle the highly perishable fruit needs to be very clear and oftentimes repeated. Jim has many stories of fruit mishandling once received by stores and individuals; this can result in unrealistic expectations by the buyer, even though clear directions were given up front. Jim sees the challenge of how to work with pawpaws from harvest to consumption to be the biggest hurdle in pawpaws becoming a commercial enterprise.[3]

When I asked Jim what cultivars he would choose if he were to plant his orchard again today, he responded: Shenandoah, Alleghany[4], Susquehanna and PA Golden.

WILD AND STRONG

One of my favorite observations by Jim: his trees that are grafted onto local wild collected seed (rootstock) can have more drought resistance than those grown from seeds from cultivated fruits. Jim notes how the trees with wild seed rootstock have stayed healthy and green, while others grown from collected cultivar seed rootstock languished during dry spells.

Pruning Notes

Jim and Donna Davis are pruning ninjas and have mastered the approach for commercial orcharding. When you are harvesting 6,000 pounds of fruit in just a few weeks' time, tree shape, size, and access make all the difference. To maintain good air flow, weight balance, and access around the pawpaw trees (which are only eight feet apart on center within rows), all limbs are maintained at four feet long or less. The sides between trees are maintained at three-and-a-half feet, while the sides facing out into the rows are allowed to stretch to four feet. Jim points out that branches longer than that get weighed down and become more susceptible to breaking, or hanging on each other or the ground. The Davis' also work with an open-vase-shape style for pruning verse the central leader approach, to help maintain a low, easy-to-reach structure for fruit harvest and ongoing pruning. Since sunscald on pawpaw fruit is something you want to avoid, many might think this is a bad move; however, the pawpaw will send out new shoots that fill in the open center and provide sufficient shading. If some fruits look as if they will be exposed to sun, then they become part of the fruit thinning. The Davis' also keep the lower branches of their mature trees pruned between 24" and 36" to maintain good ground clearance.

---

3 Selling at farmers markets can help mitigate these challenges with direct education and handling. Selling to grocery stores may be a challenge for proper handling and consumer education.
4 Though Alleghany is a prime producer in Jim's orchard, he does point out that it has high maintenance fruit thinning and fertility needs.

Thinning

Jim is serious about fruit thinning, as this helps maintain tree health and fruit quality. With productive cultivars and good pollination, trees can bear more fruit than what may be ideal. Thinning a heavy fruit load reduces stress on trees and frees up resources for healthy growth; allowing trees to overproduce can lead to early decline. Jim aims for around 35 pounds of harvested fruit per tree. Since pawpaws have brittle wood, thinning also helps prevent limb damage during storms.

Jim does the bulk of the fruit thinning in June, with a light thinning follow up in early August. He recommends starting the thinning process from the outer branches to reduce potential sunscald issues and to lessen downward pull, then continue thinning clusters down, leaving three or four of the largest fruits to thrive. See Chapter 5: Eco-logical Tree Care for more information on fruit thinning.

Fertilizing

Jim points out that there is a tendency to let pawpaw trees over-bear, which means soil gets depleted of nutrients leading to quick decline, branch dieback, blue stain, low vigor, leaves showing signs of chlorosis, and leaves around fruit yellowing.

Jim suggests to test soil prior to planting to be sure there are no missing elements; he also recommends checking pH levels, aiming for a pH between 6.0 and 6.5. In the pre-production phase, Jim recommends a balanced fertilizer of 10-10-10 with trace elements. During this phase, nitrogen levels can be upped a bit using urea. A word of caution: be very careful, as there is often a tendency toward over fertilizing. In the production stage, soil and leaf tests should be conducted to check for potassium, iron, zinc, magnesium, and calcium. Highly customize fertilizer to balance. If your soil lab does not have a baseline for pawpaws, be sure to get one from Kentucky State University and send along with samples (see the Resources appendix).

Jim fertilizes based on need while there is strong, active root growth; in Maryland where his orchard grows, from early spring through June and again in early autumn are the ideal times to fertilize. Jim avoids fertilizing in July and August so as to not stimulate new growth that may not harden off before winter.

Thank you, Jim, for being a pawpaw pioneer and so graciously sharing your knowledge and experience!

LONG CREEK HOMESTEAD, NURSERY, AND PAWPAW FESTIVAL

Long Creek Homestead is nestled in the foothills of the Blue Ridge Mountains, which is part of the greater Appalachian Mountain chain, near Frederick, Maryland. The centerpiece of our homestead is a hand-crafted, circular, round wood timber-framed strawbale home we fashioned from the woods and land that surround us.

Our 25-acre site is a woodland paradise situated along a peaceful rambling creek that offers a rich diversity of eco-zones and resources to work with and learn from. We have multiple food forests, at

different ages and stages that boast over 100 varieties of cultivated fruits, nuts, and medicinals. Our gardens are designed with raised bed swales and hügelkultur beds that passively harvest water, create micro-climates, and pump food! We grow many types of culinary mushrooms throughout the landscape for food and fertility. Much detail is given on these growing techniques in my first book, *Edible Landscaping with a Permaculture Twist.*

Though Long Creek Homestead is our private home, we also provide diverse educational offerings and events to the general public that include how-to workshops, informational talks, homestead tours, and harvest festivals. We use the homestead to conduct ongoing research into plant and permaculture systems appropriate to our climate, both environmental and cultural.

Our love for extensive plantings and research with fruits and companion plants that work well for our climate, deer pressure, flavor, beauty, and ease of care is what led to establishing Long Creek Homestead Nursery. The nursery is seasonal and has set open days from March to June and again in September and October. Our website, www.ecologiadesign.com, is the best way to stay updated on all things homestead related.

Long Creek Homestead Nursery sits in an old stone barn foundation

Open house during Long Creek Homestead PawPaw Fest

Plant wizard Eric Joseph Lewis leads a plant and ecology tour at the Long Creek PawPaw Fest

LONG CREEK HOMESTEAD PAWPAW FEST!

Our first Annual Long Creek Homestead PawPaw Festival kicked off in September 2016 with a burst of excitement and energy as folks poured in to sample prime pawpaw fruits, pawpaw ice cream, and pawpaw jam. Guests also enjoyed touring and learning about the food forests and circular strawbale home, grooving to live music, and the opportunity to purchase trees, fruit, and pawpaw memorabilia.

You don't want to miss the PawPaw Fest! Due to popularity and to keep the event well-organized, it is now a ticketed event. Updates and links are posted on our web site: www.ecologiadesign.com. See you at our next PawPaw Fest!

21st Century Homesteading

A homestead is more about lifestyle than a set of definitions or scale. Indeed, the modern homesteader can be urban, suburban, or rural. Diversity and a goal of self-sufficiency sets homesteads apart from a conventional farm.

A permaculture homestead looks to loop practices so that they support the whole "system," allowing for activities to feed into one another, as do healthy ecosystems, rather than operating in seclusion. At Long Creek Homestead, permaculture techniques include working with our woodlands to grow mushrooms and build structures, propagate perennial plants for substance and nursery sales, and create links that weave education, culture, ecology, and economy together.

Make your own homestead be what best suits you, your home, and your community.

See you at Long Creek Homestead!

Michael, Ashley, Wyatt & Baby Girl

Pawpaw Purée

★ *100% Pure* ★

KEEP
FROZEN

16 oz.

KEEP
FROZEN

Ingredients: Fresh Pawpaws (Asimina triloba), ascorbic

Made In The

www.treebornproducts.com

TREEBORN

Pawpaw Purée

RESOURCES

Pawpaw Organizations, Groups, Education, and Research

North American Pawpaw Growers Association

Pawpaw enthusiasts and backyard and commercial pawpaw growers dedicated to promoting the superior traits of the pawpaw plant and fruit.

Over the years, the North American Pawpaw Growers Association has teamed up and overlapped with the Ohio Pawpaw Growers Association[1] to educate pawpaw enthusiasts and commercial growers in successful pawpaw culture. They offer educational information on cultivar selections, planting, harvesting, collection scion wood, growing from seeds, processing, and marketing, along with other helpful information, plus many great educational handouts.

www.ohiopawpaw.com

www.facebook.com/NorthAmericanPawpawGrowers

Kentucky State University Pawpaw Program

KSU's Pawpaw Program website has an amazing and seemingly endless collection of articles, research, slide shows, and videos, among other items, all revolving around the North American pawpaw.

www.pawpaw.kysu.edu

---

1 Please note: You do not need to live in Ohio to join the Ohio Pawpaw Growers Association, as they offer services far and wide.

Peterson's Pawpaws

Here you will find the world's most delicious pawpaw varieties, together with the information needed to grow them, harvest them, use them, and sing about them, as well as many facts and meaningful trivia. www.petersonpawpaws.com

North American Fruit Explores (NAFEX)

NAFEX is a network of individuals throughout the United States and Canada devoted to the discovery, cultivation, and appreciation of superior varieties of fruits and nuts.

From their website: *Although the ranks of our membership include professional pomologists, nurserymen, and commercial orchardists, NAFEX members are all AMATEURS in the truest sense of the word; they are motivated by their LOVE of fine fruit. NAFEX members typically work together to help each other by sharing ideas, information, experiences, and propagating material.*

www.nafex.org/

The Northern Nut Growers Association, Inc. (NNGA)

NNGA is one of the longest active and most respected growers' associations. Do not let the focus on nuts throw you into thinking this is a limited resource, as they also celebrate and educate about pawpaws, persimmons, and general tree culture knowledge. The collected experience and knowledge in this association and very accessible member base is phenomenal. I highly recommend joining!

From their website: *NNGA is a national non-profit organization with members throughout the U.S. and 15 foreign countries founded in 1910 to share information on nut tree growing. Our members include beginning nut culturists, farmers, amateur and commercial nut growers, experiment station workers, horticultural teachers and scientists, nut tree breeders, nursery people, and foresters.*

www.nutgrowing.org

Association of Temperate Agroforestry (AFTA)

AFTA is a private, non-profit, 501(c)(3) organization based at the University of Missouri Center for Agroforestry at Columbia. The mission of AFTA is to promote the wider adoption of agroforestry by landowners in temperate regions of North America.

www.aftaweb.org

Backyard Fruit Growers

The informal association of Backyard Fruit Growers began in 1990 as an exchange of information for amateurs and others in Lancaster County, Pennsylvania, who wish to produce excellent fruit for the family and respect the backyard environment. Members get together four times a year at seasonal meetings

(Winter, Spring Grafting, Summer Orchard Tour, Fall Apple Tasting) to share ideas and fellowship. Members also receive a newsletter, Backyard Fruit Grower, which has a circulation of about 350. If you live within driving distance of Lancaster County, and if you would like to participate in the seasonal events, subscribe to the newsletter to receive schedules and directions. www.sas.upenn.edu/~dailey/byfg.html

Foragers and Educators

- Eric Joseph Lewis: www.facebook.com/eric.j.lewis.982
- Dan de Lion: www.ReturntoNature.us
- Dina Falconi: www.botanicalartspress.com
- Samuel Thayer: www.foragersharvest.com
- Doug Elliot: www.dougelliott.com

Pawpaw Pulp

- Earthy Delights: www.earthy.com
- Integration Acres: www.integrationacres.com
- Nash Nurseries: www.nashnurseries.com

Sources of Equipment/Supplies

- Buddy Grafting Tape: www.buddytape.com
- Heavy-duty black polyethylene tree guard: www.oescoinc.com
- Mycorrhizal inoculant DIEHARD Root Dip: www.forestry-suppliers.com
- Kombucha-making process and SCOBY providers Cultures for Health: www.culturesforhealth.com

FACEBOOK

Search the following to discover an active and enthusiastic pawpaw community:

- For the Love of Pawpaws
- North American Pawpaw Growers Association
- KSU Pawpaw
- Pawpaw Fanatics
- Ohio Pawpaw Festival
- NC Pawpaw Festival
- Pawpaw Fanclub (Europe)
- European Fruit and Nut Explorers (EFNEX)

NURSERIES

Below is a list of nurseries that will ship pawpaw trees to you.[2]

Top on my nursery list and recommendation for buying quality pawpaw trees grown in deep pots by a dedicated pawpaw aficionado is Charlie West from West Farm Nursery in New Jersey. Charlie grows out all his own seed, does all his own grafting, and ships carefully.

West Farm Nursery

116 Burnt Mill Road

Branchburg, NJ 08876

(908) 255-5471

https://sites.google.com/view/westfarm

Licensed propagator for Peterson's Pawpaws and KSU trademarked cultivars.

Peaceful Heritage Permaculture Nursery

Peaceful Heritage is a small, 100% family-owned and -operated, Certified Organic, permaculture-oriented plant nursery located in Stanford, Kentucky.

They offer Ultra Select Seedlings grown out from high-quality cultivars and a wide selection of grafted pawpaw trees. Their website, www.peacefulheritage.com, is also a good source for educational fruit-growing, advice, and articles.

Licensed propagator for Peterson's Pawpaws and KSU trademarked cultivars.

www.peacefulheritage.com

Twisted Tree Farm

Located in Spencer, New York, in USDA zone 5, Twisted Tree Farm sells select pawpaw seeds and bare root trees. Akiva Silver, the plantsman, only grows out seedlings of northern seed sources gathered from highly productive trees. His trees are one of the few sources for northern grown pawpaws. They will fare better in shorter summers and colder winters than the typical southern seed sources more commonly available. This likely is one of the most northern sources of pawpaw seed available.

---

2 For up-to-date listings of national and international nurseries that carry Peterson's Pawpaws, visit www.petersonpawpaws.com/nurseries, and for KSU releases, www.pawpaw.kysu.edu.

Twisted Tree Farm is one of the few nurseries I would recommend for bare root plant material, as Akiva is a first-rate permaculture nurseryman that pays attention to quality and proper timing. His bare root offerings are one of the most affordable options for buying quality pawpaw plants.

Check out Akiva's book, *Trees of Power*, and extensive video resources via his web site or YouTube page. www.twisted-tree.net

Edible Acres

Edible Acres is a permaculture and forest farm in Spencer, New York, that offers bare root pawpaws and a diverse array of plants.

From their website: Plants are available as bare root early spring and later fall, and during mid-season, they generally come potted in one-gallon pots filled with our own homemade potting mix rich with compost, fungal life, and biochar. All our pots are reclaimed/reused and our potting mix contains no chemicals or artificial fertilizers.

Pawpaw trees available in two sizes: 1ˢᵗ-year seedling, tiny above ground but with a substantial tap root ready to lock in to its new home, and 2ⁿᵈ-year young tree that is bigger and more developed. First-year trees tend to catch up and exceed older trees, but some people want it bigger at purchase time. The choice is yours.
www.edibleacres.org

Food Forest Farm

Food Forest Farm is co-owned and operated in Brooktondale, New York, by husband and wife team Jonathan Bates and Megan Barber.

From their website: *We sell bare root improved genetic pawpaws, along with our other offerings. The seed is mixed parentage from the pawpaw Cornell variety trials (Middletown, Mitchell, NC-1, Overleese, PA-Golden, Sunflower, Taylor, Taytwo, Wells, Wilson, and others). We grow, supply, and teach about perennial vegetables and other multipurpose plants.*
www.foodforestfarm.com

Rolling River Nursery

Rolling River Nursery is a USDA-Certified Organic nursery run by Planting Justice in Oakland, California. This nursery does in-house pawpaw growing and grafting in 10" deep tree pots, which are listed as organic on their site; non-organic listings are in one-gallon pots.
www.rollingrivernursery.com

Grimo Nut Nursery

Ernie Grimo, the owner of Grimo Nut Nursery, is the past president and a current member of the Northern Nut Growers Association. He has an amazing diversity of top-quality trees. Based in Ontario, Canada but ship throughout the United States.

www.grimonut.com

Edible Landscaping

Michael McConkey is the singing edible plantsman. His songs are as fruitful as his popular nursery in Afton, Virginia. If you have the good fortune to visit Edible Landscaping, you will see mature examples of many uncommon, yet easy-to-grow fruits to pick up for your landscape. Edible Landscaping also ships most of the year, as their stock is mostly container grown.

www.ediblelandscaping.com

Red Fern Farm

Red Fern Farm is a nursery of trees and ideas located in southeastern Iowa that is operated by Tom Wahl and Kathy Dice. Tom is a well-respected educator and researcher into agroforestry systems that highlight pawpaws and chestnuts. Their web site is a wealth of information, plus it has good genetic plant offerings, seeds, and scion wood.

www.redfernfarm.com

England's Orchard

Cliff England's nursery in McKee, Kentucky, has a very impressive collection of fruit and nut trees developed from decades of research, with a big focus on pawpaws. Indeed, Cliff is one of the most well-known pawpaw growers and has led orchard tours for many years at the International Pawpaw Conference hosted by Kentucky State University.

www.nuttrees.net

Blossom Nursery

Blossom Nursery is family-run enterprise located on the King's River in the Arkansas Ozarks. They grow native fruit trees plus other useful and unusual plants, and are especially fond of pawpaws. Blossom Nursery offers pawpaw plants in all stages, grown with an understanding of their biological requirements.

www.blossomnursery.com

Hidden Springs Nursery

Hidden Springs Nursery is a woman-owned and –operated nursery in Cookeville, Tennessee, that keeps honest roots in an industry that is fast losing its sincerity. Aside from pawpaws, the proprietors grow a great collection of uncommon, but easy-to-grow, fruits.

www.hiddenspringsnursery.com

Burnt Ridge Nursery

Founder Michael Dolan is a plantsman legend that has been growing and selling edible and medicinal plants since the 1980s near Onalaska, Washington. Our permaculture site here in Maryland is full of successfully ordered and grown selections from Burnt Ridge Nursery.

www.burntridgenursery.com

Raintree Nursery

For mail ordering edible plants, it is hard to beat the diversity and quality of Raintree Nursery. I personally have ordered from them dozens of times with good results. They also have a nursery and garden center if you find yourself on Butts Road in Morton, Washington.

www.raintreenursery.com

INTERNATIONAL NURSERIES

Florian Haller, Germany (30 km South of Munich): Florian sell seeds, seedlings in bulk and little amounts, and grafted trees—mainly Peterson Pawpaw and patented KSU cultivars. www.pawpawschule.de

- Häberli Fruit and Berry Nursery, Häberli Fruchtpflanzen AG, Switzerland: www.haeberli-beeren.ch
- Country Winery, Netherlands: www.countrywinery.nl
- Piet Vergeldt Boomkwekerij bv, Netherlands: www.magnoliastore.com
- La Pépinière du Bosc, France: www.pepinieredubosc.fr
- Végétal 85 Pépinières, France: www.vegetal85.fr
- Kobayashi Nursery Co., Ltd., Japan: www.kobayashinursery.jp
- Viher Plant, Slovenia: www.viher-plant.si
- Andrej Krašna, Slovenia: www.asminafruit.eu
- Ivan Orságh, Slovakia: ivan.orsagh@gmail.com
- Franz Praskac, Austria: www.praskac.at/obst/indianerbanane
- Lars Westergaard, Denmark: www.westergaards.dk/pawpaw

LONG CREEK NURSERY

Since this is my nursery, I cannot say enough good things. Long Creek Nursery, located in Frederick, Maryland, only grows quality plants with good genetics. We make fungal- and nutrient-rich potting mixes, never use artificial fertilizers, and focus on root health as a cornerstone to vibrant and abundant trees.

Pawpaw select seedlings and a limited quantity of grafted pawpaws are our mainstay. We also grow and sell black currants, Aronia, American elderberry, willows, and more. Please note that we do not provide shipping, so we strongly encourage you to visit our homestead and nursery in person!

To learn more about Long Creek Nursery, check out these resources:

- For all things Long Creek, please visit www.ecologiadesign.com and contact us at info@ecologiadesign.com
- Visit our Facebook page, *For the Love of PawPaws*: www.facebook.com/fortheloveofpawpaws
- Check us out on Instagram: @permacultureninja
- Visit my YouTube channel for more pawpaw ideas and how-to videos: www.youtube.com/user/ Campesinomike (or search "campesinomike" to find me)

REGIONAL NURSERIES

The following nurseries sell pawpaws at their respective sites but do limited or no shipping.

Useful Plants Nursery

Useful Plants Nursery was co-founded by one of my first permaculture teachers and inspirations, Chuck Marsh. This is a permaculture-based nursery specializing in useful, phytonutritional, food, and medicine plants well-adapted to their Southern Appalachian Mountains and surrounding bioregions.

Earthaven Ecovillage

111 Another Way

Black Mountain, NC 28711

Phone (828) 669-6517

www.usefulplants.org

Bullock's Permaculture Homestead and Nursery

North America's premier permaculture site and home to my personal permaculture heroes Doug and Sam Bullock, who propagate an eclectic assortment of perennials, shrubs, vines, and trees well-suited to the maritime northwest bioregion. (They also host amazing Permaculture design courses and internships.) Located on Orcas Island in the San Juans Islands of Washington State.

For questions about plants, nursery hours, special requests, appointments, and the like, please contact them at (360) 376-6152 or nursery@permacultureportal.com.

www.permacultureportal.com

Hortus Conclusus, Stone Ridge, New York

Allyson Levy and Scott Serrano are edible gardening ninjas who have a cornucopia of plants at their nursery, which they have turned into a publicly accredited arboretum and botanical garden. It is well worth the visit if you find yourself in the lower Hudson Valley region. They definitely have pawpaws!

www.hortus.biz

Additional Resources

Books

- *Pawpaw: In Search of America's Forgotten Fruit,* by Andrew Moore
- *The Pawpaw,* by James A. Little
- *Edible Landscaping with a Permaculture Twist,* by Michael Judd
- *Uncommon Fruits for Every Garden,* by Lee Reich
- *The Forager's Harvest,* by Samuel Thayer
- *Mycelium Running,* by Paul Stamets
- *Mycorrhizal Planet,* by Michael Phillips
- *The Reference Manual of Wood Plant Propagation,* by Michael Dirr
- *The Grafter's Handbook,* by R.J. Garner
- *The Pawpaw Grower's Manual for Ontario,* by Dan Bissonnette
- *The Pocket PawPaw Cook Book,* by Sara Bir
- *The Fruit Forager's Companion,* by Sara Bir
- *Foraging & Feasting: A Field Guide and Wild Food Cookbook,* by Dina Falconi
- *The Wild Flavor,* by Marilyn Kluger
- *Appalachian Home Cooking,* by Mark Sohn
- *The Wildcrafted Cocktail,* by Ellen Zachos
- *Make Mead Like a Viking, by* Jereme Zimmerman

Web Links

- Learn more about the Ohio Pawpaw Festival: www.ohiopawpawfest.com
- Top-working pawpaw trees: www.petersonpawpaws.com/grafting
- Earthy Delights Recipe Blog: www.earthydelightsblog.com
- Kentucky State University pawpaw recipes: www.pawpaw.kysu.edu/Recipes.htm
- Friends Drift Inn recipes: www.friendsdriftinn.com
- Alan Bergo recipes: www.foragerchef.com
- Ellen Zachos recipes: www.backyardforager.com
- Leigh Scott recipes: www.OlivetheThymeKitchen.com
- Kelly Sauber, Fifth Element Spirits: www.westendciderhouse.com/fifth-element-spirits.html
- Trevor Newman, known as The Fruit Nut, who is dedicated to exploring and popularizing uncommon and under-utilized fruiting plants: www.thefruitnut.com.
- Lee Reich: www.leereich.com/blog

Permaculture Resources	
RESOURCE	**WEBSITE LINK**
Permaculture Institute of North America (PINA)	www.pina.in
Great Rivers and Lakes Permaculture Institute	www.greatriversandlakes.org
Permaculture Association of the Northeast (USA)	www.northeastpermaculture.org
Transition Network	www.transitionnetwork.org
Permaculture Magazine – UK	www.permaculture.co.uk
Permaculture Design Magazine – USA	www.permaculturedesignmagazine.com
Sustainable World Radio	www.sustainableworldradio.com
The Permaculture Podcast with Scott Mann	www.thepermaculturepodcast.com
PERMIE KIDs	www.permiekids.com
Permies[3]	www.permies.com

PAWPAW SEEDS

- Fruitwood Nursery: www.fruitwoodnursery.com
- Red Fern Farm: www.redfernfarm.com
- Baker Creek Heirloom Seed Co.: www.rareseeds.com
- England's Orchard and Nursery: www.nuttrees.net
- Nash Nurseries: www.nashnurseries.com
- Sheffield's Seed Company: www.sheffields.com
- Dave M. Ford's Seed Exchange Mailing List: www.plantswap.org

---

3 A good online resource for practical permaculture is permies.com, which has a huge online community that shares practical and actual knowledge around a host of permaculture practices, fruit growing, and homesteading. The Permies community was hugely supportive of this manual's Kickstarter campaign!

Dru Mckenzie
Noreen Scanlon
Marn H.
Linda Watkins
Jill
Charles Best
Guest 490101066
Eric G. Rothoff
Ryan Hamilton
Don
Kyle Dougherty
Aja Jackson
Guest 1410685144
Wren Haffner
Jennifer Kunze
Philip Santay
Lisa Chumley
Guest 1455773256
Rebecca H.
Sumaya Elabi
Eric
J. Lauryl Jennings
Derryl Cocks
Adam Federman
Julie D.
Guest 205425757
David Poulson
Guest 2013454188
Sean Maky
Andrew J. Whittaker
Karin
Guest 1825574965
Tom Greenwell
Channie Wirman
Guest 1096545013
Kim Arnold

Steve Rivas
Guest 418108060
Eric J. Carlson
Darla
Guest 1587495175
Gene Baur
Linday Napolitano
Mine
Xavier Jennings
Shawna King
Guest 1489809520
Kelsey
Michael D. Wilson
Guest 382000679,
Amanda Serra
Denis Superczynski
Robert Wright
Guest 795631389
Philip Jurkowich
Tanya Sulkowski
Adam Brittain
Lauren Frederick
Guest 146017326
Steve
Chris Bupp
Daniel Ohmann
Guest 1018290509
Sarah May-Anderson
Eric Smith
Guest 1404840346
Eva Marie Taylor
Sally Willoughby
Dave Aabo
R. Shill
Guest 1217934928
Ken Lefler

Serge Rousselle
Helen Zumzan
James Brown
Guest 480455867
Eric Tolbert
Jocelyn Campbell
Craig Hockenbury
Allen Marshall
Jason Vlasak
Robert Brown
Marit Hichman
Brian Hester
Jim Doyle
Thomas Bourke
Elizabeth Brown
Guest 7059073
Over the Edge
Jason Widney
Guest 1588470017
Linda Bruno
Jeremy Irwin
Marc Brooks
Patty Friedman
Valerie Dawnstar
Nicole Robinson
Raymond Pate
Tina Tamer
Joshua Evans
Michael Tullius
Jason Williams
Sherry Frick
Guest 200455920
Lisa Landrum
Dan Ellis
Bernard Brennan
Guest 1711405582

ACKNOWLEDGMENTS AND GRATITUDE

For the Love of PawPaws Community

This mini tome is a community creation that started with 335 supporters raising over $14K via a Kickstarter campaign. Thanks to these pioneering and generous souls, I had the encouragement and responsibility to complete this not-so-mini manual.

Special Accolades

The Pawpaw Wall of Heroes (see opposite page) is a celebratory list of book supporters that sat in the middle of our 3rd Annual PawPaw Fest. It was beautifully created by **Antonette Vasseur**. Special love and gratitude out to **Todd McCree**, **Anna Chaney**, **Jeff Alvey**, **Adam Pearrow**, **Ham Sweet Farm**, and **Jerome Osentowski**, who really kicked in!

Pawpaw orchardist **Jim Davis** has long been a foundation in my pawpaw explorations and learning. Jim spent numerous hours sharing his wisdom and extensive experience with me long before this book was on the horizon and has remained a steady supporter, generously and gently guiding my journey down the pawpaw path. Thank you, Jim, for your love of the pawpaw and for sharing them far and wide.

Neal Peterson has dedicated his life to pawpaws, uncovered many of their mysteries, and joined together some of the best genetics within the species. He is truly *Mahatma Pawpaw*. Neal has been an enormous support

Neal and me at the Meadowside Nature Center Pawpaw Festival in Montgomery County, Maryland

Charlie slinging pawpaw trees in beer boxes in the parking lot at the Northeast Organic Farmers Association-NJ winter conference in 2017

to the creation of this book via numerous conversations, editing, and sharing of images. It is safe to say that the quality of this book has been greatly improved by Neal's inputs. The greatest gift, though, that Neal has given to me is the calm assurance that we are deeply rooted with the pawpaw. Neal's life and work will continue for endless generations to come. Thank you, Neal, for adding your magic to the world in such a meaningful and lasting way.

Charles West, another of our pawpaw "elders," has greatly supported this book via editing and connecting me with the pawpaw community at large. Charlie's passion for pawpaws has literally propagated hundreds of the finest trees and inspired numerous new growers. Thank you, Charlie, for keeping our roots deep with the pawpaw.

Sheri Crabtree is the go-to for pawpaw knowledge and research. Since 2004, she has been Co-Investigator of Horticulture at Kentucky State University. Sheri has been amazingly responsive to my many queries and always generous with her time and the vast resources she has helped amass at KSU. Thank you, Sheri, for holding space for the pawpaw to diversify and adapt.

Sheri investigates a pawpaw tree at KSU's research orchard

Ron and me in the Long Creek Homestead pawpaw grove

Ron Powell is the "Oz" behind the North American Pawpaw Growers Association, The Ohio Pawpaw Growers Association, and the newsletter, *Pawpaw Pickin*, along with many useful handouts about pawpaws. Ron kept track of this book amongst his many pawpaw editorials and provided helpful feedback. Thank you, Ron—the pawpaw community is much better informed and linked thanks to you.

Where would I be with my love for pawpaws—or many uncommon fruits—if it weren't for **Lee Reich**? Lee is a magician with plants, especially fruits, and great at sharing his immense knowledge. He is the author of numerous books (all recommended) and a generous donator of time to this book. Thank

Lee pictured at his Farmden (more than a garden and less than a farm) in the Hudson Valley of New York

you, Lee, for making the world a more fruitful place!

Nicole Luttrell is the talented water color illustrator of this book. Since Nicole entered our lives at Long Creek Homestead, she has helped us build our home, strengthen our edible landscape business, and edit two books! Nicole is amazing, and I am deeply grateful for all the talent and strength she has shared. With friends like Nicole, you don't need too many.

Nicole is a dynamo artist, grower, editor, and friend.

Tanner Csonka is a digital art ninja! Tanner has been through numerous iterations and creative design storms with me over the nearly two years it has taken to create this book. Tanner, thank you for your humble, yet powerful, path. It is safe to say that pawpaws have better images now thanks to you.

Tanner lives life on a creative path and translates his findings through epic digital art

Special thanks to pre-editing ninjas **Neal Peterson, Nicole Luttrell, Lee Reich, Andrew Moore, Jim Davis, Tom Greenwell, Ron Powell, Charles West,** and **Derryl Cocks.**

The final flow of this book is greatly due to an amazingly talented editor, **Wendi Hoover**, and ace book designer **Vicky Shea** of Ponderosa Pine Design. Thank you both for helping me create a second tome with such polish!

The Long Creek PawPaw Fest Volunteers have been phenomenal! The magic that happens at our pawpaw festival is a considerable force that is well-held by one of the grooviest groups of people on this planet. I think it is safe to say that volunteers at any pawpaw festival are good souls. Thank you to you all—you know who you are!

And Big Love is sent out to those who hosted me on writers' retreats: **Sivananda Yoga Ranch, Anna Chaney, Scott and Angie Ford,** and **George and Sibby White.**

MY FAMILY

Ashley Judd, my beautiful and strong wife who is anchor and strength to my fiery nature and frequent journeys out into the universe. My Goddess.

Wyatt "Wizard" Judd, a.k.a., *Lion Heart*, a courageous and powerful force of life. A natural guide.

Carolyn "Maw Maw" Judd, our matriarch who cares for many lives. She works hard to give others opportunities. She lifts us to live this precious life to its fullest.

Chris "Paw Paw" Judd, a generous soul. The gifts of his life continue to ripple and fruit—like the two "temporary" pawpaw seedlings we heeled in together 20 years ago that now produce a bounty of magnificent fruits. Thanks, Dad.

My sister, Jennifer Judd Hinrichs, large of heart (if not of stature ☺) and a prime example of putting others before herself. She walks where most people talk.

My **brother**, Jason Judd has an unfathomable mind. There are few past and present with such capacity. And he uses this wonderful mind and capacity to root out injustice and inequality. My kind of hero.

HOW TO HAVE YOUR YARD AND EAT IT TOO

Edible
LANDSCAPING
WITH A PERMACULTURE TWIST

MICHAEL JUDD

*E*dible Landscaping with a Permaculture Twist is a fun-filled how-to manual for the budding gardener and experienced green thumb alike. Full of creative and easy-to-follow designs that guide you to having your yard and eating it too!

The ABC's of Creating an Edible Landscape

- Herb Spirals
- Food Forests
- Raised Bed Gardens
- Earthen Ovens
- Uncommon Fruits
- Outdoor Mushrooms and much more . . .

Distributed in the U.S. by Chelsea Green Publishing